THE BLACK MOUNTAIN BOOK

Thick Woods
and
More Mountains

To Neighboring farms, Peek's Tavern,
The Town of Black Mountain
and Asheville

Music House

Cooks' Houses

Cesspool with sewer lines

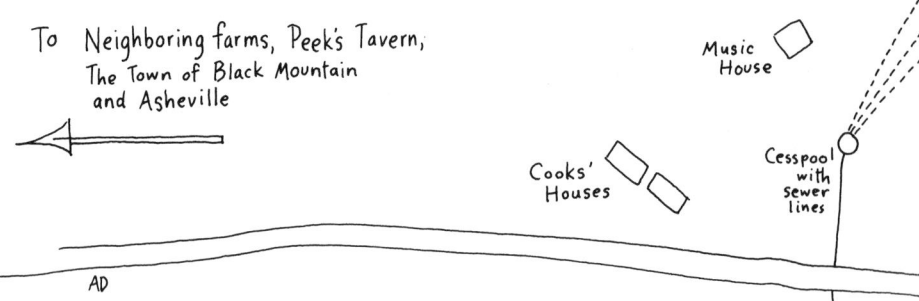

AD

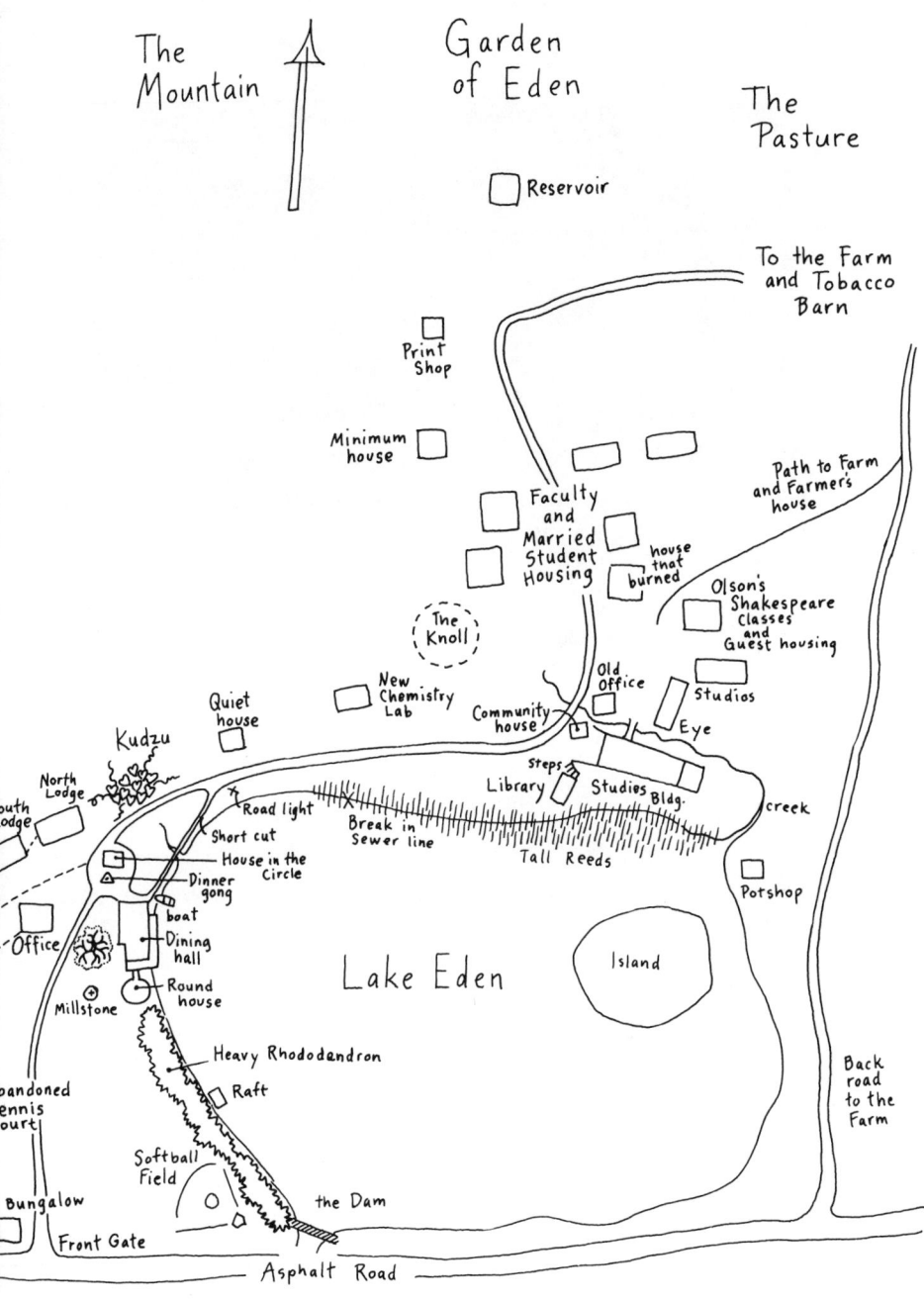

THE BLACK MOUNTAIN BOOK: *A New Edition, Revised & Enlarged, with Illustrations by*

FIELDING DAWSON

NORTH CAROLINA WESLEYAN COLLEGE PRESS

Copyright (c) 1970, 1991 by Fielding Dawson

Frontispiece: Victor Kalos and
Fielding Dawson at Black Mountain College

LC 90-62149

ISBN 0-933598-20-3

Cover drawing of Charles Olson by Fielding Dawson

Published by North Carolina Wesleyan College Press,
3400 North Wesleyan Boulevard,
Rocky Mount, North Carolina 27804

Charles Olson
in memory

"Ah…" deprecating with his pipe,
"irony is so unjust; never could abide
irony; something Satanic about irony.
God defend me from irony, and Satire,
his bosom friend."

— Melville
The Confidence-Man

George Butterick

Robert Duncan

James Herndon

Joel Oppenheimer

Flola Shepard

CONTENTS

THE BLACK MOUNTAIN BOOK (1990)

A NOTE ON THE DRAWING OF OLSON 3

INTRODUCTION 5

BLACK MOUNTAIN DEFINED 7

WALLACE STEVENS AT BLACK MOUNTAIN 14

THE LAST CHANCE 20

FOOTNOTE 22

PROJECTIVE VERSE 24

HOPE 25

DEAR CA AND BILL 26

DEAR MOTHER 30

HOW I LEARNED TO DRAW TREES 32

HOW STEFAN GOT ME TO SING 34

OLSON, POUND AND STYLE 37

THE NIGHT OLSON LEARNED HOW TO TEACH 39

PAGE FROM PATRICIA EDSON'S JOURNAL 52

TOMMY & NICK 54

MY FATHER 56

THE PORK CHOP INCIDENT 58

THE ROSE OF THE WORLD ON A BASEBALL SCORECARD 80

MY DEAR MRS. DAWSON 91

AT THE FARM 93

MORE NOTES FROM OLSON'S CLASSES 99

TO THE MOTHER OF THE PITCHER 102

YOU BELONG TO ME 105

THE FINGER 106

WHERE ELSE? 108

MY APOLOGIES 109

WOW 110

SUMMER OF '48 111

SUMMER OF '51 113

THE FISHQUEEN 115

MOVIE STARS 117

P.S. 121

THE EINSTEIN LETTER 122

FIRE, AND AFTERMATH 123

OUR WAY 124

POKER 126

WHY BLACK MOUNTAIN WAS LIKE A PRISON 132

WHY WE WENT THERE 136

LETTERS FROM MY FATHER TO MY MOTHER 155

THE BLACK MOUNTAIN BOOK (1970 *Revised*)

PREFACE   167

THE WART   172

THE HORNED BEETLE   174

THE BEE   180

THE BEE AND DAN   181

FROM ACROSS THE VALLEY   182

THE RATTLESNAKE IN THE DOORWAY   183

THE UPPER LEFT HAND CORNER   190

POISON IVY   194

DAYLIGHT SAVINGS   198

AT BOTTOM   202

DISHCREW   204

FIRE AND LOVE   205

THE LOST YOUNG MAN   244

LIST OF ILLUSTRATIONS

NICK CERNOVICH 55

CONNIE & CHARLES OLSON 66

BASEBALL SCORECARD 88

THE ROSE OF THE WORLD 89

BETTY KAISER 90

NOTES FROM OLSON'S CLASS 100

VICTOR KALOS 101

ELLEN SCHASBERGER 104

CY TWOMBLY 114

FISHING GROUP 154

JONATHAN WILLIAMS 224

ACKNOWLEDGMENTS

Some of the material in this book first appeared in the following journals and chapbooks: *American Book Review, The Chicago Review, For Now, The Journal of the Charles Olson Archives, Sagetrieb, Harper's Bazaar, Giants Play Well in the Drizzle.*

"Rose of the World" and "My Father" are from the Estate of Charles Olson at the University of Connecticut and are reprinted with its permission. "My Father" is from *A Nation of Nothing but Poetry,* published by Black Sparrow Press (1989), George F. Butterick, editor. "At the Farm" originally appeared in a different form in *The Sun Rises into the Sky* (Black Sparrow Press, 1974).

The photograph of Betty Kaiser is reproduced with the permission of the photographer, Charles Archer.

The photograph facing the half-title page is reproduced with the permission of the photographer, Andy Oates.

The letter from Alfred Einstein and the photograph of Charles and Connie Olson are reproduced with the permission of the North Carolina Division of Archives and History.

The map of the college was redrawn from the author's sketch by Ann Di Salvo.

THE BLACK MOUNTAIN BOOK (1990)

A NOTE ON THE DRAWING OF OLSON

In February 1956, while staying at Franz's studio, I received a letter from Jonathan saying he was going to publish the second volume of Olson's *Maximus Letters* (11-22), and would I do a drawing of Olson for the announcement? W.C. Williams had made a statement and Jonathan wanted a drawing to go with it. I showed the letter to Franz saying I could, as I had often done, draw Olson from memory, so Franz gave me some paper, ink, a brush, and after a couple of tries, I did it. Showed it to him.

He smiled, and said what he often said about his own work, or a work that pleased him, which is how I — and quite a few others — learned to use understatement.

"Pretty good!"

INTRODUCTION

The first edition of the work to follow was begun in March, 1967 and completed in September, that year. It was published in January 1970, the same month (of the same year) Olson died. Not bad. *On* target. He had been humiliated by my Franz Kline Memoir, published in November of 1967, and had written me not to use his name again.

So.

Croton Press was the imprint. Harold Witt publisher, a Wall Street broker and sort of poet who, as these creepy crawlies never fail to do, published a book of his own poems, somewhat like James Laughlin. Michael Perkins was editor, Connie Avon Art Director. Paul Bacon did the drawing for the cover, which, although I had wanted to do my own, I liked, and enjoyed meeting him in his studio, to supervise minor changes. He was one of the more talented artists in that field.

The book sold, not big but steady, and a little money made all round. Harold was difficult, like a damp mattress, to wring royalties from, and in so few years, in one more example of publisher irresponsibility — another of all too many — Mr. Witt got bored with it, and closed down his house, leaving — considering his brief list — some pretty good books (and writers) to fall by the wayside. Including, for which I'll never forgive him, Donald Phelps' brilliant volume of essays, *Covering Ground,* a book selected by Pete Hamill (in *The New York Post),* as one of his Ten Best Books of the Year (Christmas, 1969). Large and small, so easy for publishers to be the uncaring human machines they can be, as they talk about money, it's not money, it's how they are, *that's why:* they're *cold meat.*

So it is an honor, and a warm blooded thrill to take a professional, long overdue revenge in this just right, introductory spot.

F.D.
May 21, 1990
New York

BLACK MOUNTAIN DEFINED

Black Mountain was freedom.

And within that freedom I and others developed a discipline in drawing and writing that involved listening and seeing with such continuous intensity it became my way of life. As much an influence on me today, and every day, as it ever was. Black Mountain was not something you grew out of. Like freedom, you grew into it.

The pure, open space we lived every day, was a *lot* like Paradise: not involved in the accepted world, the understood geopolitical sense of reality.

Black Mountain was the people who were there, which explains its sudden changes. From 1950, or for sure '51, it was Olson's until it closed. Very different than Albers'.

With its lake, farm, mountains, shingled lodges and buildings, in its community way of living a lot like camp, in both senses, but as Dan has said, the school was the people who were there. It had an organic understanding of itself being transient. People came and went. The list of famous names of students and faculty (that I am sick of), gives a false — wrong — impression, that leaves, however, a lasting mark. Too bad, because there were all kinds of people there. And all those are ignored, Harvey Harmon, Tim LaFarge, Andy Oates were Black Mountain, like Victor, Nick, Phyllis Franklin, Trueman McHenry a real *nice* guy. Peter Nemyni, who studied physics with Max Dehn, and went away to Princeton, around 1950, sad to say goodbye yet so happy, yet so sad. Leaving Black Mountain was tough. One didn't do it every day, one didn't want to do it at all. Ever. We said goodbye to Nick in front of the Dining Hall — no! Outside North Lodge, across from the gong, and rear entrance to the Dining Hall. We embraced him, and Herb.

Seeing the car go down that road, a vivid identity went out of my life, that day. Without Nick, the school would adjust to itself, which was its style, with a vital organ gone. Yet he had to go. I knew the feeling. I was next. I had come alive in Paradise, I'd changed a lot, matured, but I had to go. Students and faculty on me, I was getting too good. My drawing and writing were indeed good, maybe too good, maybe those people were right. Well, too bad for me. I was drafted.

The basic, most accurate criticism of the school, that it was out of touch with reality, not involved in matters of the world, is true. But that's all. Nothing else can be said, there is no other criticism possible. The people who manipulate the school for their own advancement, who never went there, misunderstand that criticism, valid then, still is, always will be. Inside that criticism, like a little vein, is a tone, an aura, a note, of jealousy, and it has that vindictive, creased tinfoil quality where freedom equals irresponsibility: don't want too much.

If you went to Black Mountain from July 15th, 1949, until it closed, you learned a lot about art and its various forms, you learned nothing about the Real World. Black Mountain it was true, did not prepare you for that, and this point of view has a lot going for it, but quite a lot not. The Reality and World defenders are arrogant in their reach, and intent. They mean that Black Mountain being out of touch with reality and the world, nullified and ignored it. Wrong. Black Mountain was a place of its own being, like freedom, it didn't nullify or ignore The Real World — it was away from it. The world wasn't there, like the other side of the mirror, or beyond the horizon (that fascinated Melville [and Olson, and me, and Black Mountain]), every aspect intangible, invisible, except the lush natural Paradise that it was.

People who didn't go to the school will never understand that like freedom, the school was atemporal, which gave it its transparent character.

If you didn't look where you were going, at Black Mountain, you might not know where you were. It was of the very essence of dreams. Other aspects — its fossil and mineral life — lent an air of Before History. In its boundless, often difficult to contain sense of discovery, Stan Vanderbeek whittled the bamboo pens he used to draw and letter with. Students cut the collars off white dress shirts, dyed them fuscia, chartreuse, for a trademark, like the logo on school bulletins: a circle within a circle, bringing cows down from the pasture, Vic Sprague (biologist), and his quart Mason Jars full of Georgia Moonshine, to the tune of a thousand frogs, and crickets, as I gazed across the lake deep into the night, talk of reality, and the world.

The story is within the crystal, not without. All the interviewing of former students and faculty, including a book and exhibition of our works of art, are but shallow reminders, dim reflections. It is too bad, and may seem unfair, but so Black Mountain was, and if you *weren't there you will never know, or understand.*

Unless you create it. That's the catch. If you never were there (or were!), and write it, you'll have to create it. If it is about it, it won't be that way it was of it. So, in the original Happening, as Mary Harris documents, Cage's stepladder, radio, dogs and dancers production at school — summer '48 — Cage created it. So too must it be written.

There was no pretending: we walked into it, located ourselves, and began the assimilation. Thus we became it, and were free for an unprecedented involvement in the arts. Lou Harrison taught his students how to compose music, but he also taught them to perform, *and* to conduct! And this, where all the arts overlapped, went on and on and on, each of us at the top of our form, again and again, and feel the slow change, so as the pen touches paper and the hand moves, you are within the crystal, and without looking at the paper you draw the model, Joe Fiore had told us, don't look at the paper.

The model — Bea Huss — put on her robe, and I looked at the paper and learned by not looking at it I had achieved a line that appeared more fluid, for my eye and hand were so disciplined to look from model to paper, model to paper, in that rhythm, it had become a routine, meaning to me slick. The direct result of Joe's classes is my staying on the rough side of things, meaning the experiment continues, I am yet within the crystal, and I am still free.

There were people at school who remained alien, but important, for they reminded us of the Outside.
 And certain people adapted faster than others. You would think I did, but no. I had been in two locations quite like Black Mountain, in early childhood. One place in Florida. A beach, oceanside. The other in the wilds of Pennsylvania mountains, so at school I had to learn where I was.
 There were three approaches to the farm. One from the asphalt road (leading in from the highway). One from the same dirt road that you entered the property on, it continued on around back, and the other was in heavy undergrowth, behind two wood frame, shingled houses, across a small clearing and over a bridge above a deep creek. I went to the farm by the back road once or twice, in my four years there. Never went by the asphalt, always over that bridge, but I must have gone to a place very much like that somewhere else, before Black Mountain, because after I left Black Mountain, I forgot how to get to the farm. I did a lot of work on the farm. That farm means something. In my dreams I get lost, and wake up not knowing where I am. Black Mountain was powerful in that deep elusive way, intangible, out of bounds and flowing free, touching on logic without being of it, the serious illusion that kept what it was not, poised, on its own threshold: bringing to dreams what the dreamer could *never* believe, making before and after I went to school stages in the same dream, meaning another aspect of the crystal was the persistent and odd, but not unpleasant feeling, will I ever wake up? *No.* The section of the road from the Studies Building to the light pole, and the shortcut to the Dining Hall — with the lake off to the left — was like a tunnel which,

right. And, that fall, a new student, in pottery, showed up who was also gay. His name was Kitty, and after that Paul Goodman summer, several of the boys, and as if overnight, or on cue — the girls, too, became interested. So the school, adjusting to itself, went on as usual with new distinctions made. We teamed up according to compatibility, not so much as lovers, although true in a couple of cases, more in terms of communication. Who you could talk with. In that wonderful way of Black Mountain, most people understood what had happened, not because they were good people, and they were, but because they were interested, say what you will, it was an interesting situation. All those macho guys.

It was a character of Black Mountain — a trademark — if things didn't work they did somehow, so an across-the-board switch to a gay boy and girl element in the student population (what, forty, fifty, then?) rather than being the exception, became another part of the pattern, arrangement, composition, in and of the school. On the surface nothing changed.

It was always of its own process. Always. The summer of 1952 was legendary yes for the future big names that showed up. But for those of us who had tested ourselves, at summer's end we knew that perhaps in secret, a phase had ended, and Black Mountain moved toward new changes, continuing to define itself. In July, Jack Tworkov and his wife, Wally, in particular their two daughters Hermine, and Helen, brought new vitality into the crystal. The next month, August, Franz Kline was there, himself a crystal. M.C. Richards wrote the lyrics for *A French Farce Based on a Wagnerian Opera* in which the entire school, save just a few, participated. Saying goodbye at end of that month was sad, it was true, but the school was poised for its future, that fall, as a new batch of students arrived, including some girls.

WALLACE STEVENS
AT BLACK MOUNTAIN

No, he was not there, nor would he have been, the way things were. But he was taught there, although not by Olson. I suspect Olson had not read Stevens, or if he had, not at length or in depth. But there are poems by Stevens that had Olson given attention, might have influenced him. Note W.C. Williams on Stevens...see the opening lines of *The Kingfishers,* and those of *The Blue Guitar.* While he was rooting around tall grass and Mayan ruins in Yucatan, M.C. Richards was reading Wallace Stevens to us.

I had for sure never met anyone like M.C. Wearing men's shirts open two buttons down. Soft, worn jeans. Mexican sandals. Lined, experienced face. Thick, dark hair in page-boy cut. Spoke with gestures. Enjoyed exaggeration. Theatrical. You knew how she felt. She touched, could bowl you over. Me over. And did, too. Eyes got that gleam. Big Grin. Big. Face very expressive. Smoke? Wet, then wrapped her lips around a Camel cigarette, tilted her head, took the light you offered her — face intent — inhaled. Deep. Raised her face said thank you. But I was never sure who I'd be looking at as she raised her face, for it had changed from the way it had been. I was very young, very naive, but that I felt she put me on guard with this ritual, and kept me there, seemed an essential stance for her. This memory speaks, saying I like and love M.C. We share many memories, most of which are vital, reveal differences, some are great just the way she said it: that's *great.*

She had a grand love for theater, the world *is* a stage. Always was. Will be. She looked across the classroom table, her dark eyes getting bright. Amused. She knew. She *knew* I had never, ever heard anything like this, never heard ANYTHING like this: looking at me, not at the open book on the table, before her. Quoted the title, and read aloud, the first line of a poem and the first line was the same as the title, which puzzled me as I watched a hand put a Mason Jar in pine trees, in Tennessee. That's what she read. I placed a jar in Tennessee. Sat back with a big smile, cried —

"Isn't that GREAT?"

"Yes," I answered, amazed. "It's *terrific!*"

M.C. stands for aspects of the school that left untouched render it academic, while being modern, avant-garde, experiment in community, etc. She was in both a formal and informal sense — in action — able to translate and interpret what Olson meant to both the faculty and students AND, one in the same, able to do both to Olson, often to his annoyance, if not anger. Before the faculty at large, in social situations, or in the ultimate small group, of three. I had written him a long poem, at the end of the summer of 1949, about a kind of existential lawnmower, cutting its way across the universe, which I gave to Olson. M.C. was there. Outside the front door of the Studies Building. Olson looked at it — it was long and very, very bad — I was so anxious I couldn't stand still, just able to breathe, so jumped around, frazzled and miserable as he it was clear did not know what to do with it, so gave in my misery, the poem back to me.

"What are you doing, Charles?" M.C. asked.

He didn't know what to say.

I didn't either. Just nineteen.

"It's a poem," she said. "Fielding wrote it for you." Her voice got an edge. "Don't you think you might keep it, and read it?"

"Yes, of course," Olson whispered. Whatever happened to that poem shall remain a mystery. I think it made its way back to me pretty soon, and in my humiliation I threw it away, but M.C., standing up for me that evening, was a pal, painting an interesting little portrait of Olson who, in the heart of his galactic fireworks, didn't have the common sense to thank a young student — whom he liked — and insert poem in back pocket. Tell youngster he'll read it later. It meant he was still the academic big shot, who drove down from Washington, D.C. Later Black Mountain knocked some common sense into him, a lot in fact.

M.C. had again stepped in during one of his classes, that summer. He talked of *Patterson One and Two,* and Pound's *Cantos.* I had never heard of Williams, nor Pound, and laughed out loud, in spite of it, for to me it was as I said, on being asked, by Olson, what, was funny? Bill Bill, I responded, Ezra Ounces. Scattered smiles around the table. Olson annoyed.

"Can't you see it from *his* point of view?" M.C. asked Olson. "Their names *are* amusing."

The breakup with her husband Bill Levi, who went to Washington University after the final, devastating faculty fight in or around 1951, taking their young daughter Estelle with him, made things difficult indeed for M.C. From her point of view that period at the school was perhaps the lowest, for her. I've heard no one discuss it, no doubt to her relief.

The transition period from Albers to Olson, from July 1949 until what, fall 1951? difficult for anyone to bring into clear, fair, focus. But for me, it was the closest I got to M.C., not too much in a personal sense, as through her classes, as I'm sure Russell Edson, his sister Pat, Harvey Harmon, Jack Boyd, Cicely Shellhase would agree: M.C.'s Joyce class a real whiz, as it was there that I latched onto Faulkner, as well, meaning large sources of influence on my work. These sources were until the winter and spring of 1951, the most profound, until Melville's *Confidence-Man,* and not long after, M.C. to my amazement, confessed she was jealous, which I could *not* figure out, until she told me, in my study overlooking the lake, one afternoon, she was jealous of my not having yet read *Moby Dick,* to read it for a first, which I've never forgotten, to a point where it's the same, *Moby Dick* and M.C.'s honest announcement, which I have used since, for I found out what she meant, in its truth, that, next to *Don Quixote,* unparalleled initial experience.

We must rid our minds of the famous names that have come to identify the school. A fresh approach to comprehend and define

Black Mountain, would be to place M.C. at narrative center, and define Black Mountain through her. She as much as anyone, far more than most, assumed its identity, absorbed it, no matter where she was or is, and in spite of any denial — even hers! — standing or walking, she loved to walk (and stand: vertical woman), smack dab in the heart of the crystal, with Wallace Stevens in her hand, she thereby becomes an essential image and leading character of the school.

With Olson in the background.

See?

But not quite.

For M.C. was a paradox. For all her vividness, was in part hidden. Divided. Maybe with a public/private personality. Could be. She gave off the image of faculty, while also that of being a student. Youthful, enthusiastic, formal, aloof authority. Imaginative. Literal-minded. A woman in man's clothes. Regarded as liberated, today. Didn't shave her legs, or under her arms.

Her involvement with pottery which began at school, began her life or at least renewed it, for it gave her a tangible, dimensional richness that replaced writing (until she wrote about pottery). The texture of clay far removed from the close, even ominous fact of writing (look what she had to write), could well be seen as a threat and besides, pottery was a *lot* more fun. She loved having fun, and laughing. Doing both, very compelling. It could be that one of the few one-sided, rather unfair, even cruel, aspects of Black Mountain was its pressure to work. Olson, in his constant seriousness didn't know what it was to in continuity laugh and have fun, and in our likewise severe peer group pressure on ourselves, there was heat on her to write, and I recall her saying she was working on a "long manuscript." As in *shhh,* it's in the works.

It defines Black Mountain that she gave off the illusion that she was intuitive. Sly. Could see what was coming. Not so. Not one bit intuitive. Took things as they came. Was easy to surprise. A pushover. But clever enough to act both. I liked that, understood it, but was more intuitive, which is why she kept me at a distance.

I liked sly pushovers. She made sure to be decisive, firm. One or the other. I can't recall her being both with me. With others yes. Charming, fun and funny. She touched. But very much a tactile person, anyway.

And a loner.

After the class finished reading *Dubliners,* she gave us the assignment to write a paper on it, which I did within a day or two, and handed it in. Was about two, maybe three short paragraphs, and one page long. I tried, but couldn't figure how to stretch it out, so handed it in with an apology for its shortness.

Very unlike me I can't recall the location where the following scene took place, because am sure what she said overcame where we were. I wrote in my paper that on the first page of *Dubliners* a young boy was looking up into a window, and on the last page an adult man was looking down, out of a window and M.C. said I had stolen that. I said I didn't. She asked where I had gotten the idea. I said I didn't know, it had occurred to me, after having read the book. She said — she did, too — that she didn't believe me. James Joyce's brother, so-and-so had written Joyce a letter saying what I had written, and Joyce had written his brother back saying he was right.

"I didn't know that," I said.

"The book of letters from Joyce's brother to Joyce is in the library," she said. "You went there and read that."

"No I didn't."

She held up the paper. "This is what he wrote."

"I didn't know the book was in the library," I said. Nor knowing how to behave.

"Well it is, and these are his words, which you copied."

"No," I said. "I didn't. Honest."

She turned her head, gave me a cynical sidelong look, while she weighed matters.

"I don't believe you," she said.
I didn't understand. "Why would I do that?"
"I don't know," she admitted. "But you could not have written this on your own."

Meaning I was a cheat and a liar. But she was a fool. Why would I cheat and lie over something like that? Because she looked through academic, faculty, literal-minded non-intuitive eyes, teaching me a lesson about M.C. which may pass for whatever it may be worth, until the recollection of one more incident, and this in class. Story in *Dubliners* about the two boys who what, skip school, and encounter a man with "bottle green eyes" who, at the high point, walks into the distance across a field, does something fishy, and returns to the boys. M.C. was mystified by what the man did, so far away, and I wondered if I should tell her. She asked us if we knew, and people muttered and such until it seemed so obvious. I didn't say jack off, I said he masturbated. M.C. flushed crimson, negative. No! *Not* what Joyce meant! Missing me telling her that me being a jack-off artist, I knew what it was, and that's what the man did.

"Look how he changes, his personality changes afterwards, after he — " I paused, while she didn't get it, " — after he has orgasm." I felt like a dummy. But, the others in class came round, and in discussion it was taken as one interpretation. M.C. embarrassed, maybe angry. And not long after, I turned in my one-page paper.

In writing these I realized that the concept "within the crystal" comes as result of my receiving Stevens' *Collected Poems* as a gift, while thinking of Black Mountain in terms of film, as definition, to cast light on a period of the school's history with, as I discovered, M.C. the lead character, the definitive identity, I recalled her reading aloud the first line of the Stevens poem, the "jar in Tennessee," being a neighbor state to North Carolina, my "crystal" is but a translation of his glass jar located so few actual miles apart. So a further discovery in kinship is made, in them, of them: M.C., Wallace Stevens, and Black Mountain College.

THE LAST CHANCE

The last thing most artists want to do these or any other days, is to challenge, or threaten, the system. With few exceptions artists are bound by their egos and ambitions, competing in an arena of theatrical, unimaginative imitations of endless Impressionism.

They think if their work is on exhibition it is therefore good, original, vital and important art: this is the true aesthetic of Capitalism: important because it is being seen (a basic rule of advertising, show it often enough and they'll think it's real. The way they sold us Reagan, the way they materialized the shadow Bush), no matter how amateur/fop or empty, or what pale icing it is.

Black Mountain was the last, the final creative process that saw, from its Bauhaus roots, in a dying comprehension of individuals removed from money, possibilities in advertising. By considering this in terms of our own work, however, we came to understand that if we didn't make it, in that world, we couldn't imagine the men who would, because we were too creative to be able to. We offered the last "maybe" — the finest art we were doing — check the names of us who were at school — the last chance for a creative approach to corporate greed and the power men to stop in their tracks, and reconsider.

In the early Fifties the Container Corporation of America presented, in an ad, a brilliant water color by Philip Guston which stunned us, and we saw — it could be done! Was there hope? Could it *be?*

Of course not.

But our interpretation, and high ideals, were based on an innocent vision of our own work. We saw what we were doing, and we were doing just fine. Hoped it might have an effect — and we were right. It did. We did! Olson at Black Mountain first perceived the destiny of poets as distinct influence on the culture, which later in his Buffalo years flowered.

But, rather than a movement, it went one by one of us, that did, without a group dynamic, and always within the system, meaning we were (and still are) a vital part, but a healthy part, or air, a fresh breeze in a vicious, ironclad racist brutal Nation of Greed changing only for the worse.

FOOTNOTE

Reading George Butterick's Introduction to *The Post Office*, we learn Olson was ambitious over possible publication, and sent its three sections to *The New Yorker*, which were returned (as they do) within the week.

Beyond that effort, he was intent on getting down the details regarding, to the extent he wished, his father, in a way of thinking that's what writers do, but having a correct hunch he was writing a literary obligation, we note he never wrote on those matters again, meaning after magazine ambition and literary duties he was free to pursue what he wanted that year (1948), and, through the encouragement of Dahlberg, Olson went — he had been invited — to Black Mountain to lecture on Melville, meaning that in this way he took a step into his future, and left a past behind him that concerned him being "a writer" which he had, as George notes, called himself: he went through the experience of being a writer and came out a poet.

But he was his kind of poet, and one that, in his way had such a love of narrative he never dropped it, but bent it, snapped it in two, or three, composed and rearranged poetic lines on the page according to his passion, and never far from the continuous feel of discovery, it runs through his work that within one narrative should run another.

He couldn't achieve this in prose for he had been bound to a single-minded journalistic mode that was how writers wrote and, because he feared to bring to narrative his whole attack, it would upset everything he couldn't comprehend, which anyway would take too long, and might yield chancy results, at best.

But the wish for a doubled narrative never left him, and if not in obvious evidence, it is this that makes his later work so solid in texture, oak gone out of sight for he gave to image a single doubleness he'd held in the 1940s for prose, and because he didn't blow it all out in prose (the organic failure of journalism), it held firm in the sweep of his work, for the rest of his life.

This explains the counterpoint beginning of *Call Me Ishmael* (the *First Fact* section), and the mysterious lines on Fernand in the opening stanza of *The Kingfishers,* and throughout, perhaps here and there (*O'Ryan* meaning Orion), becomes his psychic glue, his love for and faith in proper nouns, true source for mystery, a la Frank Moore, to form the root of his familiar, total imagination.

But it comes from the movie *The Lady from Shanghai,* the sequence in the crazy house, where Orson Welles walks in a visual Surrealism, with its exaggerated effects, while his voice-over tells the whole story of the beautiful lady killing the men she did, and very poignant, in his Irish accent: *walking in a forward moving narrative* hit Olson with a wallop: the past was being verbalized while walking forward — a famous scene in film lore, which everyone has been drawn to, in particular as it precedes the house of mirrors shootout, with Everett Sloane on crutches. And of course Rita Hayworth. Olson, like all of us, fell for the same things everybody else did in movies, and the crazy house sequence was if not a lasting influence, the original jolt, for it brought into focus an unusual double articulation that we at once see yet also hear, and follow, spellbound.

It is true, in life, we hear and taste and see and smell and feel all at once, but it is not, was not and so far as I know, will *not* be on the calendar for future poets and poetry, as it was for Olson, and still is for me.

PROJECTIVE VERSE

I went into the Studies Building, and saw him standing by the mail boxes with some papers in his hand, and his face pale with rage. He didn't see me, but yelled a curse over my head out the door into the sunshine, and smashed the letter between his hands as he clapped them, and cursed again, circle-eyed, cheeks taut with fury, exhaled a cry, The sons of bitches stole my word.

Stood there, gazing out the doorway, and repeated, The *filthy* sons of bitches.

I checked my little cubbyhole for mail, there was nothing, and rather tiptoed down the corridor, leaving him there…fat chance. Still pissed off, no kidding. I hear him. Yes! *Listen.*

HOPE

After lunch, sitting around drinking coffee on the porch, another golden day in Paradise, the lake seemed to rise into the sky, and the grand Blue Ridge Mountain Range tilted toward a future no one would dare. I loved Faulkner, and quoted a famous passage about hope.

Olson made one of his breathing scowls inhaling Fuck hope, exhaled, and glared at me and not a pat on the back for me, nor to imply that I was to be ignored (fuck off), but not to let me just be, either, therefore trapping me. I was shocked, hurt, astonished and puzzled. How could anybody be that way about hope?

DEAR CA AND BILL

Dear Ca and Bill,*

I'm having a wonderful time here just as I told you in the first letter. Yes, Mr. Kean has visited, and with him was Dr. Penniman. They came last night as I was working on a mural. They told me that they would come later to visit some afternoon.

Well, brother-in-law and sister, a few things have I on my mind and I want to tell you them.

For one: the girls around this place, not all, but a good many, use terrible languadge. Now, for a male to say son of a bitch and for a male to call another a bastard is o.k., I can see that, 'cause I do it myself; but, for a female to drink gin and to call the guys she's with dirty names, why I just can't see it. For that, one of the guys called me grandma and pious and whatnot, so, you see the kind of people that are here. Even the teachers use bad lingo. I don't mind some of the words, but when you get into the vulgar in teaching a course, why that's bad for one thing, and it's unecessary. I'm sure you agree. What would you think of a man, a very brilliant one, who uses the obscene to teach a course; well, not to teach it, but, well, you know what I mean...

I like a girl to be decent and a fella too...my vision of a college boy, is one who leads a decent life, swears, drinks beer, that's o.k., but these guys, just because they're labeled artists, drink gin and swear, and the girls do too...maybe I am too prissy, but nevertheless I don't quite like it.

There's one guy here who is wonderful Ca, his name is Arnold.

---

*A letter to my sister and her husband, postmarked July 12, 1949. The letter is printed here with the writer's original misspellings and other errors.

And, he's a cuban, I think. Anyway, he's wonderful, and he paints. He reminds me a whole lot of Billy, not only in his manner and ideas, but in his personal appearance. He slicks his hair back exactly the way Billy does his, and he has that same nose...and it's nice to have one person down here that reminds me of Bill, don't you think so?

Gee, this guy Arnold is smart too. He knows his painters right and left, his writers and men of the country in politics the same way. I haven't seen any of his work, but I know that he can paint and create very well, just by his personality.

Now, this other guy, Hank, or did I tell you about Hank, well no matter. He is a commie sympathizer. And on the first day I arrived he began to tell me some of his ideas. And not so surprising, his ideas haven't changed one little bit, I mean he hasn't changed one bit, he seems like a guy who learns one thing and can't learn another. He hasn't read but one or two books of Wolfe, but he talks like he knew the man, and he has the gall to tell Mr Olson, (the Verses and Drama teacher) that he likes Wolfe yes, in parts, and that his description is good, but he gets nowhere...ahhhh, nuts. I'm getting all mixed up, I wanted to tell you about something which seemed to me wonderful about this guy and now I'm all mixed up.

Hank thinks just about all people who believe in the Christian God are either, crazy or prissy. Many of the students feel this way. Sure, I should overlook this and say that it is part of the school and that is the reason why the school is so good, because of the free thinking. But, I can't help feel, that if the students were all Christians...think of the wonderful stories and paintings and verse and drama and ideas and creative ability in all fields that would come out of Black Mountain College then...why, even the thought makes me happy!

Well, to hell with Hank, I want to tell you about Mr. Olson. He is...gosh, words fail me...about ten steps higher than stupendous. He is about six feet eight or nine and has shoulders like an ox. He must weigh about two hundred and sixty or seventy. He eats, well, let me tell you about last night's meal when I went in and sat by him after everybody else was through and he was talking to one of the students.

On the table was a plate that had about five hot dogs on it. Another plate had about ten buns, another had heaping piles of tomatoes and lettuce, and then there was another that was stacked high with potatoe chips and oh so many more food.

When I left, everything was gone except a few pieces of casual leftover lettuce bits. He thrust his face within about six inches of the girl who he was talking to (hey, I'm fifteen minutes overdue for lunch, I gotta scram, finish later...) (Sorry kiddo, I have nearly a half hour more to write, I though lunch was at 12:15, it ain't, it's at 12:45)

Anyhow, Olso picks up a hot dog, breaks it in half, smears one end in a mess of mustard on his plate, takes a bun rips it in two and then into quarters and then into very small bits. He takes a gargantuan bite of the hot dog, crams a bit of bun in, reaches across the table, grabs a slice of nice red tomatoe, pushes this in his mouth, still clutching the outer edge of the tomatoe, bites down on it and his paw returns with a little pale red dripping of what was once a tomatoe. Then he scrapes up a few fingers full of potatoe chips and he squeezes these in his mouth. Then another bite of the hot dog, etc...All this time telling about Howard Fast, Saryon, Ezra Pound, T.S. Eliot, Thomas Wolfe...etc...and smoking a cigarette and drinking a glass of milk!

Well, that's Olsn. He doesn't like Thomas Wolfe, Saryon, Scholem Asch, Irving Stone, and I am very disappointed for I thought sure, just one would suit his taste. I asked him the other night,

"Mr. Olson, how do you like Wolfe."

"No good, bad on public morals."

"Saroyan?"

"No good."

"Scholem Asch?"

"No good."

"Why?" He saw the questioned and puzzled look on my face and he said, "Every dog has his own fleas."

Then he turned and walked away laughing very loud.

He read us something of Carlos Williams who was writing about Ezra Pound, and when he hit something funny, he (Olson) would begin to wheeze, and then out he would come with this great torrent of laughter, mounting higher and higher and louder and louder till cresendo. A roar like a lion. Believe me Ca and Bill, that man is huge, like a giant, and he is as wonderful as he is big.

When he said to me about every dog having it's own fleas he bent over and rested his elbow on my shoulder, inhaled a tremendous drag on his cigarette, winked at me and said, "Every dog has his own fleas."

He likes Ezra Pound very much. We are, at the end of the year, going to three plays, the first, our version or interpation of Homer's Oddyessy; the part about the cyclops and Ulysses. The second (they are all fifteen minutes long) will be a selection of Ezra's and the third will be something we can make up, our own creation.

Doesn't it sound wonderful? Gosh, I'm overwhelmed...then think of the painting and the sculpture, I'm taking, and the Hindu Philosophy, and the French...? Boy, it's over my head, but it's still wonderful.

I think this letter is satisfactory, and I'll write again, tell boss, that I loved his letter. Am working on an oil painting and have done a few sketches of the teachers and students. Have a picture of Buckmister Fuller which I'm sending mother; see it, you'll like it. Egad, I'm so very happy......so long kiddos see you in (maybe the fall) I might be able to hop a ride with one of the teachers maybe...

So long until then
Fee

DEAR MOTHER

April 9, 1951.

dear mother:

    thanks for the letter and allowance. today the brooklyn dodgers came to play the asheville tourists, the local ballclub here. carl and tim and webber and joel and I went to the game. it was real great! the dodgers won: 9-8. as you know the dodgers have several negro players. 2 of them played today and one of them, roy campenalla, got two home runs. he is a catcher. the other, jackie robinson, a second baseman, got a home run. all the kids in the park cheered for both campenalla and robinson while most of the older rooted for the home club. i heard no remarks from any of the people around me, but joel said that there was a guy that talked about niggers etc., so he and tim and webber moved down where carl and I were sitting. the game lasted four hours. we got home just in time for supper. it was the strangest ballpark i've even seen! it seated about 1500 people and there must have been at least 5000 that came. ½ of them were negroes — more about that later. in the first inning asheville scored 3 runs. in the third they scored 4 runs. brooklyn scored 3 in the 4th inning and 3 in the 5th. asheville scored once (on a homer over the centerfield fence) in the sixth and brooklyn scored 3 more in the 7th inning. people, little kids, dazed looking, washed out, dressed up, faces roamed back and forth. I've never seen such a restless crowd! kids ran all over the playing field. once a ball was hit into centerfield and the brooklyn (duke snyder) ran back to pick it up and he just about beat six kids to it. for obvious reasons negroes weren't given seats. they stood on the left field line about 400 thick, when jackie robinson got his home run which was inside the park, a great fat negro lady ran and took his photograph. when roy campenella hit his first homer the same lady ran right up to him and took his picture. on his next home run she ran right up to him, took his picture, tore off her hat and leaned back and yelled! everybody in the stands nearly died from laughter. it was so funny. you would have loved it. asheville is in the class B baseball.

the book I sent for got here today. it looks good. i'm glad to have it...you know what i mean.

everybody is back from spring vacation. classes began this morning. i hauled rocks as i told you, and it certainly took some of the fat off me! my back is a lot stronger now.

so long, tell the family hello for me: fee.

HOW I LEARNED TO DRAW TREES

In high school I irritated my pals because I stayed home nights to do paintings of trees.

I loved trees, and on those long teenage walks late at night, I stood against trees, embraced them, and napped among their roots, to feel Him.

But the trees I drew and painted were awful, ugly green blobs above brown mush, and I almost wept. I couldn't *do* it. *Get* it. Make it, *paint* it.

But later, one afternoon at Black Mountain, Joe Fiore told us — his drawing class — we were going for a walk, and draw trees. Imagine my surprise! TREES! I'd tried before, at school, to draw and paint them, and bushes, too, but had the same bad luck.

So we walked up the road, drawing board, sheets of newsprint, ink and stick (I used sticks as well as pencils and pen, in ink) (India), in hand until we came to an area where we could spread out and Joe said okay, go ahead. Look at the bark.

I got it.

I drew the bark, I drew the branches, leaves, the tree. The paper was too small, but I knew what I was doing and I drew the roots, the trunk again branches of course every vein in each leaf. I drew flowers the same way, and blades of grass, insects, even buildings (Ben Shahn had taught me how to draw bricks, not difficult, I'd done construction work): I drew the interior of a leaf, letting it spread outward, to the edges of the paper. I drew up, along the stem, in the center of the page (of a sketchbook), following the veins outward, they, my guide toward the whole form on the limitations of the page, reverse of outline. I drew the inlines.

The months of drawing Greek Meanders had paid off.

Several years later, in New York, my friend Maxine encountered DeKooning on the street, and they strolled over to her apartment (Second Avenue and 13th Street), for a cup of coffee ("That's all. Just coffee."), (Franz hit on her if I was out of town. Those guys!) ("No Franz," she said she said.), and seated at her table having coffee, Bill saw the drawing I'd done of her, framed, on the wall at eye level, there.

"He said you're a draughtsman," she smiled.

In those days there was no higher compliment. DeKooning — those fuckers could *draw*.

HOW STEFAN
GOT ME TO SING

Wes Huss was the Director of Theatre at school (I see his wife Bea, baby in arms, crossing the field in front of the Lodges), and when he decided to produce Brecht's *The Good Woman of Setzuan,* he cast me in the lead, and we had some nasty tangles. But he was persistent, ever see him use his charm? Don't miss it, one of those directors who can act. Cynthia was to play the opposite lead, and be my love (she was anyway, despite the violent affairs she had with Tommy Jackson, Tim, Victor, Dan, and Creeley [before Jorge]). I accepted. Although angry, didn't mind playing the role of a pilot, but I was also to sing several (no less), songs, and I hadn't sung since church, in Kirkwood, Mo. I was in a lot of plays in high school, but I hadn't sung on stage — *ever,* so being as I was *going to sing,* I would go to Stefan for lessons, everything being decided for me, I went along. You know, until the curtain went up and I was on stage, and but for the prompter the play would have been the utter disaster I in part wanted it to be, because I *hated* it because it *embarrassed* me. And in the beginning I trudged up to Stefan's house, with a heavy heart and a head full of gloom. Hilda opened the door, cheerful: amused. I went in. She (academic or not, she was young and there wasn't a straight guy at school who didn't miss seeing her go by), turned, gestured to Stefan at the piano, and departed.

Their house had two stories, wood frame with shingles. Nice. Up the road on the side of the mountain.

I crossed the room to him, who rose from his piano (grand), and greeted me. Typical: effusive, head tilted, eyes bright, big grin.

Arms out, fingers spread, seeing I was nervous, assumed a look of amusement, and slight reproach. Said I was nervous and I was nervous, said not to worry and I was worried, said he'd help me to learn to sing — we, together. We would do it together. Sit.

I sat.

A small stand on top of which was a large plant, on a large, round copper tray, to my right. In the front room. Good-sized with windows. Sunny. Stefan very happy there.

He had written music for the play. Wes had decided not to use Kurt Weil's.

> On a certain day
> As was very well known...
> The poor woman's son
> Will gain the golden throne

Stefan at the keys, I, dutiful, beside him. He began to play and sing the above lyrics, and as I could read music (Dan was teaching me trumpet), I read along, hummed a bit. Louder, he said, so I hummed louder, then sang, a little, and he said louder, stronger, so I kinda did that and he got up, reached across in front of me, took the plant off the copper tray and put the tray on top of the piano, put the plant back on the table, sat down and began to play telling me to sing loud, and strong, which I didn't do and he stopped playing, turned, put his hand on my shoulder, and said Fee.

You must, he said, SING! Whereupon he turned, and as both his hands hit the keyboard, he began with that sort of yell he had ON A CERTAIN DAY, AS WAS *VERY* WELL KNOOOW-WWNNN...

Sat back. Laughing at himself. Looking at me. I nodded. Unh huh yeah right, almost blushing in amusement and fright. He sat forward, fingers struck the keys, I sang pretty loud LOUDER he yelled and began singing again as I sang louder, but still self-conscious and he yelled SING FEE, *SING!* Which I did, a little louder and then some, but still — he stopped. Jumped to his feet. Grabbed the copper tray, and holding with his left hand smacked it with his right BOOOONNNNNNNNNNGG shook the whole house including foundations, LIKE THAT! Put the tray on the piano, sat down, glared at me, began to slam out the music. I began to sing. I mean, I sang. STRONGER, he yelled, and stopped singing, but kept playing and I began to yell and I mean I *yelled* that song JA JA he laughed as I cut loose, THAT'S IT! — a force, a call I never knew came out of my throat, I saw his face shine, as he played, and I sang, until the song was over, and we fell silent. He began again and I sang along, loud and strong GOOD GOOD he cheered, and finished he began again and I sang with him, clear through, I loved it, and after I'd finished, Stefan sat back, looked at me, expression warm, tender, triumphant.

"Good! See? What a good voice you have!"

I might have reddened. I'm sure I did, in my pride. But I acknowledged what he had said because it was true, and it was Stefan who had done it.

OLSON, POUND AND STYLE

Olson — first and foremost — learned how to write the way he wanted by writing. And he never stopped writing. It was always going on. The switch from prose to poetry was because he was learning so much he had to change the layout of the poem on the paper so the writing would fit.

He read a *lot*. Voracious.

He had a memory second — if at all — only to that of Franz Kline — both men recalled things said in conversation, with tone of voice highlighted, and geographical location an essential character.

The descriptive nature of prose wearied Olson, because his interest was information, nouns. He had a love of narrative as great as any reader, but not as a writer, thus created a kind of poetry or verse to allow an unlimited memory packed with libraries of information the page-space to actualize it.

His writing of the 1940s, after he got out of politics, forms his new foundation as first a writer, second as a modern stylist. His life before can be seen as development in character, and as fascinating as it is, with his fate as his shadow, right on his heels, the friendship with the artist Cagli, Olson's struggles in prose, the seminal poems, his *Call Me Ishmael* — all like a great stud, champing at the aesthetic bit, frustrated and angry, desperate for a style that would not only work, would fit yes his needs, but would become his delivery.

Most important of all.

And in retrospect, in a countdown, with Black Mountain getting closer and closer to him, we are fortunate to have another excellent book: *CHARLES OLSON & EZRA POUND: An Encounter at St. Elizabeth's* by Charles Olson. Edited by Catherine Seelye.

First hand, this fine editor's documented, and perceptive *Introduction,* followed by Olson's own reports which he calls Cantos — there are 10 — plus Notes and all kinds of things with a LOT of information and scholarship, throughout, right there between the lines, Olson developing through prose the style he would lift from the lips of Pound and take away as his own, his way, as no other style would, or could fit, his delivery in poetry. And it came through Pound's speech as well — if not more, in fact. Also his personality where Olson realized he (Olson) was the more powerful man, — Olson was the heavy.

Admitted Pound was one of his fathers, but in describing Pound being charming, the tone is of Olson writing of his father, in *Stocking Cap.*

The real fathers don't just "go away."

One future day a group of interested persons will do a study of 20th Century poets, which will include the Imagist Movement — and should discuss the powerful reigning literary magazines and groups. In the Seelye book, Pound discussing the Bloomsbury poets and writers, is fresh, stimulating. Olson's descriptions of Pound stunning. Called him a lightweight. A tennis ball. No kidding.

Olson took it so far — farther than anybody I can see — he opened language out to fit into thought, and made poetry the process whereby thought arranged its place and destiny, on paper.

THE NIGHT OLSON LEARNED HOW TO TEACH

The first year I was there, from 1949 to 1950, Olson commuted from Washington, D.C. Began to teach in the fall of 1950. He read our manuscripts aloud, before we discussed them, and before he began to talk about what was on his mind.

At the beginning there was an awkwardness, for he wasn't altogether clear what he should do, or how he should proceed with us. This was how he got in trouble with Mary, by reading a poem by Mark, and saying she had written it. Certain folks are still sensitive. A *lot* of very creative people at that school, many have long memories. Writing this in the summer of 1989 and through May, 1990, recalling Mary taking Olson to task is a vivid memory.

He left for Yucatan somewhere late 1950, and came back a few months later. Was there in the summer of 1951 — the Ben Shahn/ Robert Motherwell summer. He had known Ben in D.C. during their Office of War Information days...1951 was an odd, difficult summer, as the year before it had been. I was so young, and ignorant. You write your book and say I was this and that, to me I was ignorant. I had failed many classes in high school, there were worlds I didn't know. I was intuitive, very talented, had a good ear, was a natural, but in any discipline I was terrible. Every teacher I had told me so. Talented, creative with no discipline or hard knowledge.

On Olson's return his classes began and went as they had, through the summer, into the fall (1951).

The late spring of 1950 I had written a story called *Father*, which appeared later in *The Black Mountain College Review*, edited by M.C.

The many months Olson was away, she was my writing teacher. And the two years, 1949-1951 into the spring of 1952, the school was very different than anyone has depicted it, going through a transition, and seeing who was there, becoming an extended male/female homosexual experience which would indeed be a book in itself, as well as a brilliant film, noted elsewhere, to not be about the school but to define it. I think we were courageous, do have sad regrets I was so mixed up, for it was a daring, poetic, dramatic and original experience. The tone of the first edition, with Kitty, the parties and Maypole dance, was in its initial draft too hot...I was very much in love with a lean, clean, red-headed Lesbian who, in her way, also loved me. A few years later I met a gay woman in Germany, and we became friends. She had a Mercedes convertible, we drove around Heidelberg on afternoons and to a party or two out into the countryside, at night. Had it not been for that sweet lady at Black Mountain, the German experience wouldn't have been what it was...in 1957 I wrote a one-of-a-kind story called *Bloodstar,* concerning the red-headed woman at school and the other in Germany who becomes the narrator, before the giant from the tower, who confronts her on the steps to the castle, at the end, speaks to her.

I have an affection for frail and insecure people who act tough, and the lady at school no exception. In my innocence, never having met anyone anywhere like her (still true), she had me spellbound, yet lest I lose sight of things as they were, while it was true of me being as I was, she presented a false front to me because she had to. I remember too well the compelling women she wanted, and her coming from D.C. (which later I came to know, visiting Ken and Neil Noland), and do remember her — she was not only tough, but sophisticated and cruel, cool, too: she hunted day and night, in particular at night, the way it was in buildings at night, things closed in, and a stillness come down from the mountain, with an echo in it. We knew where each of us lived and, in a vivid sense, how, so to be alone with someone else, where you lived, was an outrageous act for we all lived alone (exceptions don't count), which is why, better than a novel, or novella, even a stage play, a movie would be ideal. The way we saw each other, and as I saw her, in someone's doorway, as I passed by, her back to me, in a semi-profile the light of Vermeer, smoking her cigarette and speaking, in a low persuasive voice, to the other woman inside, unseen. I knew who it was.

It would be a rich, sweet personal (one more) revenge on the ambitious unspeakables who never went to the school, pretending an involvement, *daring* to assume it, in a pose for all to see, getting the facts right, and the big, famous names, with lots of photographs, while in one flat deadfoot strikeout, they missed its heart, its spirit, its sex, its madness and original creative, deceptive power.

The theme for the film would be the Scriabin Piano Concerto.

The thought *tantalizes* me.

She phoned a few years ago, saying she'd read a review of one of my books in *The Washington Post*. I asked (I knew), had she bought the book? No. We laughed. She liked the review.

I drew and painted, and wrote a lot. And in October 1951, I wrote a story called *Mother* (unpublished until here), and aside from *At The Farm*, the only other that concerned daily life at school.

I took my new story to Olson's class, and as things got going and he read our work aloud and we discussed it — our responses were good. But in reading my story it was clear it was wrong for him, and at the passage HO HO HEY DROP, with the following attempt at word/sound dramatic effect he stopped, tried again, but became so self-conscious he stammered, so I — embarrassed — said he had the rhythms off. Baffled, he tried again but couldn't, and Mary said, I can hear her — why not let Fee read it?

I hear her say that because the previous year, 1950, at a student reading in the Community House, I had read my story *Father*, just written, out loud to assembled students and faculty, scared out of my wits as I did so, and to unexpected applause I stepped aside to let someone else read. But the next day in the Dining Hall kitchen, back by the window near the sink by the stoves and rear entrance, Mary, in a soft voice, of surprise and awe that I won't forget, complimented me, for I was just twenty, and she used the word writer.

Next year, in Olson's class that night, I took her suggestion, and after my story was handed from him, down along to Nick, Joel, Mary, Duck, Victor, Cynthia — to me, I read it the way it was written.

From there on each of us read our own work, and we all discussed it, before Olson read his work, his newest poems, which would these days be understood that it was his show, those classes, those nights, but not so. As he read and later lectured, to develop his formula for teaching, we listened and at certain points asked questions, which kept him on his toes, too, attentive, and alert, to respond.

MOTHER

As in a dream he stood by the crib while the baby shrieked. Monday. Monday is a metaphor. He was exhausted because he had pitched hay all morning and at lunch he told himself that he would not return to the field to help that afternoon under any circumstances. But he did. He returned to the farm's fields to pitch hay that afternoon not because he wanted to — at least not for that alone — but he returned because there was something to be done there and he could help do it. Sitting at the lunch table (he remembered) telling the old lady:

"Oui, Madame, je suis fatigue... je suis *tres* fatigue."

He reached the field and she stood brownshouldered laughing there in the sun as he came. They worked with the tractor. The tractor would not run. The truck would pull the haywagon. He stood in the sun beside her talking of the work of the day. Everything was ready. They worked. Her face was red from the work. The wagon filled. It was hot.

One load. Another. He and the other: the redbeard, raked and scattered hay in the loft as it came up from the wagon, through the window, running down the track, stopping : clank! : and the hay falls onto the dryingramp where the two boys rake it off. (One of the boys quit working because the claws frightened him. It was true.) As he shoved the hay off the covered ramp he felt his back and shoulders and arms fumbling weak : not working. Then they were through. Driving down to the dininghall he sat beside the driver. Driving down to the dininghall in the green armytruck he watched the boydriver, he watched his eyes driving, looking, his pointed eyes : pointed : ahead : driving. That night they sat laughing on the porch. The beer came and they prepared for a party. They drank. The party was a flop. Nobody was in the mood. He stepped on one of the boys sandled toes for the second time that night. The party broke up. Everybody went to bed. He caught up with the others and he stepped on the toes for the third time.

He sat outside on the bench waiting. He was a babysitter and he had forgotten. Mother was at the show. It was almost twelve. He waited with furious anticipation. Then the baby cried. don't stick her put it on the dresser there dampdiaper other pin easier. The diaper flopped free from kicking legs. The baby screamed and sweating he talked to it. He tickled the baby gently : he was afraid of her. use the cottonballs youll find here dip it into the oil here and wipe her off you wont have any trouble this shouldnt happen this never happens only once it happened it wont happen again she sleeps like a log. He dipped the kleenex into the mineral oil. He couldn't find the cottonswabs. Lifting the legs, he gently swabbed between her legs, but the baby did not stop crying. He flicked the perspiration from his forehead with his finger.
awwwwwww now come on baby
He bent over the crib. Mother went to the show. He fumbled with the diaper. dont stick her jesus red bloodbubble pop dark on white skin. He felt the baby's skin. now after you do that she should be allright all you have to do is wipe her off a little and then put the diaper on like this unfold it lift her legs bring this part under her bottom and then bring this part up between her legs and then pin

it together here on both sides there. Shriek. The baby gasped for a moment, stopping to gather in air, and then shrieked. He felt her tiny hand clinging to his finger falling asleep with my finger in her hand? Sneezing and choking the baby screamed continuing that series of shrieks that mount past perception, that permeate into the body with the ease with which perspiration leaves the body and just as that water is wiped away then, so it returns, and so as in a dream he stood by the crib wiping away the uneven hoarse shrieks from the field of his forehead that rose studded with crystals of sweat from the fences of his eyebrows to the curving expanse of hair above and so they returned and so he stood with his eyes closed and his mouth closed too, as in a dream, by the crib. Then he looked down at the baby rolling about there and he did not hear her and he disbelieving, reached down to touch her; he touched her and his hand recoiled back and he heard her coughing screams. He touched her again. The diaper was wet. He took it off clumsily. he waited . the other stood across the left from him but more to the front . it came up : CRASH : it came towards them above : arm raised to signal the other to yell : they waited waiting : coming down there it came moving to them coming
HE FLAGGED DOWN HIS ARM YELLED HO HO HEY DROP DROP DROP DROP whhhhhiiiiissssshhhhhooooouuummmmmmp! stabbing pushing lifting pulling heave pull heaving heavy hay stabbing the pitchfork in pushing down firm lifting too heavy too much heave drag pull towards me grabbing the fork down by the prongs with the left hand regardless of blisterpain and holding high on the forkhandle with the right pulling with left stepping backwards dragging tripping dragging towards me blanket of hay moving slowly soft ssssuuuuk sound coming now the blanket of hay moves pulling sweatsoaked back belly face covered tear sweat gasping wet pulling je suis marie JE SUIS MARIE JE JE JE JE SUIS MARIE turning away from the crib he ran out of the room, through the other two into the hall, through the door into the lobby dank smelling lobby to get him the other to come help and into the room lying asleep should i wake him? shake shoulder shake : shaken

shoulder body whirls up shaken WHAT! WHAT! shrinking back muttering carrying spoken muttered apologies WHAT! pointed eyes point points the wrong boy the hay lifted up and returned to the field   stumbling against the wall feeling the rough grain on his shoulders dragging into the bathroom seeing the figure sitting there the messiah there and he sputtered out that the baby is crying, saying that the baby is shrieking and that he had done all he could do, would, and would he please come, I have given, I have done all everything, would you please come he would the messiah nodded yes, yes, he answered, ok he said, all right he sighed : I'll come.

FROM NOTES TAKEN IN YUCATAN, APRIL 13–14, 1990

It has been written that we worshipped and imitated Olson, our Master, and so it may have appeared AND in truth, may have been. I'm not sure if I worshipped him, I sure loved him, but that isn't why I imitated him, which I did.

I did because my personality was unformed, and so was my style of writing, to which may be added that what paternal worship there was was tempered with awe *and* anger: *my* father had died, and on this next father-round (with Franz coming up), I was cautious and frightened for my own skin (self), while suffering from a self-consciousness and bad stammer and, being unable to find release through crying, which I could *not*, I felt a continuous pressure, and terrific conflict: everybody was smarter but nobody (to me) understood me, a problem from which Olson kept a solid, 30,000 mile distance.

So, as it always happens, for something must occur, I developed a migraine headache which lasted for many weeks, say a few months. Nothing phased it, and my only consolation, and source of empathy was from Connie, saying Olson had the same in Florida, and one day, going into the ocean for a swim, bam, all of a sudden his sinuses emptied, and standing, waist deep in the water, it filled both his hands and he had *big* hands. Which shows how impressed

I was, having no memory of the end of my headache, I recall his. Yet, knowing what caused my migraine at school, I wonder what caused his, in Florida?

I imitated Olson's style because I didn't have any. I did the same with Melville's *Confidence-Man*. I imitated Faulkner, and Joyce and D.H. Lawrence and William Carlos Williams (later Raymond Chandler, Dashiell Hammett and Ross McDonald).

But art, any art form, in unstated declaration — a rule, a law — demands commitment, and as I had in fact arrived at Black Mountain having more or less certified my commitment, was prepared to follow, no matter what, which is right away why so many gifted, more talented characters beg off, for the demand is too great. Enter the ambitious mediocrity, eager and willing to follow through. They are the best sellers, the rich and famous, painters, movie people, etc., and always will be, those arrogant, sleazy insecure ass suckers.

So, if you're young and talented and you've made a commitment to an art form, the first step toward your own style — how your work will be recognized — will be through a direct imitation of another admired artist.

The second step is the following through, taking what you've learned with you, but developing in spite of many mistakes (most from lack of thought), a prototype of your own, which is composed of its own voice, and tone, of style. This second stage lasts almost all artists, of every kind, their lives. The third step, which even Mozart never reached, is the creation of a new style from that prototype by breaking free from it. Olson came very close. So did Franz. But Guston made it. The only one so far. Perhaps the hand that holds this pen, that writes on these blue lines in this Marble notebook, while sitting in a wooden chair, at a wooden table, facing the beautiful Caribbean, across the peninsula from Olson in Campeche, 1951...maybe this will make that change, too.

Nick told me I didn't know how to listen, so I worked on it, I began there, at school — giving focus on remembering what other people say, as well as recalling my own tone — difficult, *very* difficult at first because, in my innocence, I regarded my intuition, and ability to change, as escape, like I had in high school, and I had to learn that both were entrances, open doors, *into* the process. An uphill, bootstrap task.

Each of us and make no mistake about it, Olson too for in truth he was not yet the Master, we followed a certain range of interests along a similar path, but in varying degrees, and with different results. Olson maybe in another way learned more than all of us and it is a sad, dreary shame that George Butterick isn't alive to hear these words: Olson had learned from us, yes, but it was on an intuitive level, not quite conscious, where he, and we *were learning how to learn,* that he got used to and so did we: for it to work for him (and us), we had to know how to listen — so did he, and there was no other point than the point which varied class after class, that we go into, we got right into it, and stayed there. Thus developing an intuitive discipline that has served me (for one) all my life. And this is the reason no one has written any kind of real book on Black Mountain, because these writers, the *them* people are WAY WAY *WAY* too conscious.

In brief.

Olson's feel for the concept of space was complete, fitting the man and wanderer that he was, and finding in the Mayan ruins clues to a civilization he regarded as potential alternate to that of the Greek, he had come full circle from the space he intuited in Melville and, like reality realized, at once his own.

In a way of puzzles no one has brought this to the foreground, that the school and what was going on in New York was a distinct, even obvious, harmony, drawing as they did, on each other.

In April of 1953, on my visiting Franz in New York, as I've written, he took me to meet DeKooning, and having just shaken hands and Franz mentioning I was visiting on spring break from Black Mountain DeKooning said he had been there in 1948 and of a sudden we were talking about the school, and DeKooning talking about Olson. Had I read that book on Melville, no not yet but I would, DeKooning's yes yes hint of impatience, hit, I say, in his eagerness to express how it interested him, in no detail save tone of voice and that was PLENTY! because it was reflective because it was touching an intuitive area DeKooning was familiar with.

The energetic atemporal.

To Jackson and Franz it was innate, a given. To me, too. And Olson. (And Whitman, Melville, Parkman not to mention the Indian tribes and, lest we forget America the slavemaster, the intuitive space from Africa. We are indeed still, a big country made small by tiny little bits of thinking, almost none original.) (To say almost is to be kind.) All of which has been unseen, ignored, and for damn sure forgotten. All of it.

Nobody knew what Franz meant saying he couldn't "get into it" or, "It won't let me in." Standing in front of a painting on that paint wall we built, I knew what he meant and never thought otherwise. The painting wouldn't let him in. But in writing these new reflections, I saw that of course, no one was seeing the obvious, as, by the way, is usual, as regards the critics, and their busy busy little media.

Franz went into a variation of Third Eye frame of mind, pure thought, wherein the process of *where to put what how*, came alive in *all of its many different possibilities* including, in some instances, a lengthy and complex but quick-witted process of elimination toward just the right move (which established would create more possibilities). Chance was a big factor (which Pollock said was not true in his work), to be used, or taken advantage of, only if it fit, and if in a sweat, paint was applied and it didn't work, and couldn't be scraped off, the painting might be lost — ruined. The awareness of wrong moves matched, even superseded, that of the right ones... people are amused at Franz's famous line, "Nobody cares about being right anymore." This is what he meant. Oh yes yes, in one's life, making decisions, etc., true. But in his intuitive working, being right there inside it, and getting it right was a thrill not many people even in the arts experience. Franz was unique because he had lived at least a couple of lives, and was also an artist. Which is the precise reason he and his work are unseen and without fail misunderstood: the lives he lived and their different stages were reflected in his work , which through his being at one in the paint, on that canvas space, through his intricate, selective spontaneity, the artist transformed himself into interrelated images, in his art every bit as complex as himself. His studio space became electric, I know. I was there. And as he made small lines perfect, brightened light areas and darkened dark ones, he hummed, because he was happy, because he was right, because he was bringing the work into completion. In this way, if you give it a chance, as you look at it, let it come to you. Don't think. Open out and let it in, and listen.

There is no melody. It doesn't have a tune.

But it's him.

Guston was very impressed, awed, mentioning seeing Franz's painting *Laureline,* where the black paint had dripped, run down to the bottom of the canvas and Franz, seeing a possibility from the accident, added more paint, allowed it to run down, too, turned the canvas upside down, stepped back to see (he hadn't seen it: in catching the accident was working blind — in pure intuition), stepped back into a focus where he saw the lines running up to the top, liked it *and* how it affected the rest of the painting and, stepping forward brush in hand, formalized its completion.

Guston of course knew what had happened. The painting said so. I knew that too, which is why the memory is rewarding, because it's what Franz did, which is what we were doing.

In Joe's drawing classes at school, I learned how to look at a blank piece of paper until I saw the place where I would begin. Olson's classes were like that as well, in listening (I wrote "Olson's classes are like that…"). So it was how we were and regarded each other. The dialogue and discussion is impossible to recall because it was on that level, although some is remembered. Watching Olson as well as listening, he very near drew the language, and in the sum of sections of *Maximus* and the bulk of all short poems and fragments, in writing this while facing the beach and water as breezes ruffle palm trees, I have the feeling he wanted to break poetry up, apart, open it out and reassemble it in a more irrational, chancy vision. It may be true of the later work, in those fractured street-like grids and underlinings, but it may also be my own desire for such a narrative, heretofore unwritten, but the wish, the desire, feels his.

At no point since I learned it has my brush or pen touched canvas or paper without my knowing where to begin, which was and is in essence, an act of composition. One mark led to another...it still does. Always will.

In this way or approach, through its discipline, all of M.C.'s writing on pottery, and the pottery itself, is her book on Black Mountain.

I learned to know where to begin by allowing a disciplined and knowing eye to discover, and be at ease there, to witness and believe it as it beckoned.

It is every possibility everywhere beckoning, to the studied, wise eye to see, and hand with brush or pen to touch the space of canvas, paper, or wall. It is music because all art is impossible without music, and for that reason it is theater, like life itself. And in imitating our masters, Franz, as a younger artist, in the tough, lean, mean years of poverty that drove his wife mad, in the sign painting, barroom mural period where those sweeping brushstrokes held in context of the figure, he imitated the signature — his initials F.K. — of Tolouse-Lautrec — T.L. — within a circle. The F backward, in an act of self-deprecation and humility, for he loved Lautrec because Lautrec could *draw* — and it is that grace, even beauty — that gave style, character and a kind of fastball class to the name KLINE, freed from the circle, which still, and always will, stand for intuitive originality. Just as the two-edged satire in the signature P. Guston, and the ambitious thrill in *deKOONING!*

I didn't know, or realize, how much I learned at school until I wrote this. Yes, it was rough around the edges, and it's taken a lot of livin' to find out. The one thing we did not have in the 50s was the words to speak, to tell what we were doing. But we did *all* the rest, except — again — be able to answer Harold Rosenberg's repeated question:

"Does anybody have any ideas?"

In the crowded Cedar Tavern. Nobody could answer because we were doing, and not thinking, and Harold's astute query predicted from that point on that critics would speak for the artists, and in magazines and books circulate (and establish) labels that define over and over just who was doing what in their newest work, while along the way, ever resentful, and jealous, happy happy to empty their intellectual bladders and bowels on persons (me), and things that got in their way, like Black Mountain: as free as flying babies to shit all over us and it is *still* true, all that blather to compensate for personal creative ignorance in terms of drawing or painting, or even how to see, and sense the space and free release on a piece of paper, in tar splashed on a sidewalk, or torn posters on long cement, wood, or stone, or brick walls there in the city, or outside the city, of any city, anywhere in the world, and I hope these words bring alive the verve, the fresh vitality in space, in our composing atemporal images, finding a new, vivid, rewarding — great doors opened — freedom.

PAGE FROM PATRICIA EDSON'S JOURNAL

dear fee?
    i am not sure, and i don't know anyway, i am eating almonds and drinking what seems to be left-over old mission from last night's cloudiness....it is in a small joanhellerglass...joanheller was not there but i drink anyway....merrycaroline's room was filled with me last night plus some others that i will not bother to define.and before that we went down to mrspeeksplace to pick up some beer..thoughtless of me perhaps not to let you and your sister know but by then i was a little stewed and didn't remember...why didn't you come into my room after you knocked/i would have given you, (if you wished) some o.m. jorden and (I) were just talk-talking.so anyway i didn't go to bed early as you thought...didn't you hear the comotion in mc's roomlast night i brought her back some beer 1 and someone else did too and then we drank and even paul was there and even frankjoelnormandorothea et al.....timmerryl....the wine which i have just sipped is verry sweet..do you believe me?please come to my room and we can have some...its a secret,nobody knows i have any left....they think i used it up last night so i will not be bothered by (friends?) now that i am empty,....? of them i am not thinking of them but of myself yes and of you yes yes and no too...but of course you understand that i am not myself as always i feel a lonely lothing and a bit ofwrath toward some but i shall collect myself when and if i can see my family..then i can return new...but even if i do not return we will know that i know some things that i never knew before..i do not yet know their names but i feel them which makes me know that i will know them and i do know them. yes there are things..yes and i

accept them too..do i accept you? i don't know yet but do you suppose i should? when there are other things that i am not sure of yet but those are answers that will come if only i can go home home and see those others that i must admit i love. o'there are so many other things to say...to regain a lossness that i must regain to pick up some lost strands...then the identity of the poet is...the "is," or "whatness" counts. is that too deep for all of us? i don't think so.., well i drank last night with mc. and i like mc. i know mc. and i venture to say that i like mc. very much.....and there are others. my pen reminds me of geneva where i lost its twin and where i remember things i loved. pat

p.s. i wore my other hat the little old mission-colored hat but only because i have a cow-lick not because my hair is short, which used to be my reason.

TOMMY & NICK

Tommy, with his long, kept-trimmed blonde hair, and woman's hair brush in the glove compartment...MG convertible at stoplights looked in the rear view mirror, and brushed, and brushed... center of Asheville. Barefoot, too. And at school, in jeans and shirt (tail out), kept the brush in his right hip pocket.

Image: Paul and Vera bundled up in the front seat of their Army surplus Jeep. All flaps closed. Dead of winter and the world his track. But Vera never got her due, or our thanks...creative, talented, high energy person.

If one person could be Black Mountain, it would be Nick. Dan says he thinks of him, these days. Me too.

But I also think of Mary. Yes. Mary.

NICK CERNOVICH

MY FATHER

My father was my father
but my mother was the moon
She I have but he
died too soon

So I must be my father
— double up —
and catch all things
in one silver cup

He used to sing
he used to play
he used to hammer
and walk all day

She made me young
she made me gay
she made me turn
the other way

He used to whistle
he used to laugh
he had to do both
— he dare not cry —
he was a calf
and very shy

I liked his heart
I liked his eye
I liked his sense
of the other guy

He had a smell
he had a breath
he was sweet
death, you cheat

I had a father
he died too soon
I am lonely
me and my moon

   CHARLES OLSON
   March 4, 1945

THE PORK CHOP INCIDENT

1.

If someone was going to be late for a meal at Black Mountain, it was customary for them to ask a friend or loved one to save a serving, which was done by putting the plate of food, covered with another plate upside down, on the overhanging metal shelf above the stove where it would keep warm.

No one would steal it. No one. But to not steal it was an act of honor, a sacred honor — for we were always hungry, and there was never enough food. There was plenty of milk, though, and Wonderbread, butter and peanut butter and I believe on Saturday afternoons — lentils. And when the lentils were gone, back to Wonderbread, butter, peanut butter and milk, day in and day out. But to steal someone's meal was unthinkable. Un, and I mean it, thinkable. One boiling hot summer afternoon we risked Joe Fiore's fury by breaking into the walk-in refrigerators and stealing — and drinking — the six cold bottles of beer he had (on trust) put in there, for himself. The beer was delicious, and he was of course furious, and though we had made ourselves scarce afterwards he soon discovered we had done it, and in the inevitable confrontation it took a lot of pleading, and begging to his understanding that we had to do it: the day was very hot and we couldn't help ourselves — *cold beer* in the refrigerator! we knew it was his, but it was beer, and cold, and we agreed had it been ours we too would have been outraged, we admitted we were sorry, we apologized, we would never do it again (he never put his beer in there again) (in fact he did, with the understanding that our lives were at stake), needless to say his reaction to our regret and promises, or to the obvious fact that plenty more cold beer was available at Peek's Tavern, but he didn't want to drive five miles in and five miles back to enjoy the beer he'd already paid for, as of course we were all broke, so not only had we stolen his beer — the beer he'd paid for, he was broke too, but we couldn't replace it, the matter never was settled, although he did drive in and came back with some beer, we were nowhere to be seen, Joe had a temper, so on the purchase of his second round, we hoped he enjoyed it, and no doubt he did, with a certain lethal pleasure unpleasant to us! there in so small a Paradise stealing our teacher's cold beer, he whom we saw at almost every step of every day, just as we saw ourselves, not to mention seeing him in his drawing class, painting class, the weekly classes we had when we viewed each other's work, or the visits he often made to our studios, as well as at breakfast, lunch and supper, and on top of all that — we had broken an honor bound school law — no stealing. But, being locked up in that mountain valley circumstance, aside from breaking a law and an honored tradition, we had stolen drink, and it followed that if drink was scarce enough, which it was, it was suicide to steal someone's meal, set aside, on the shelf above the stove. I often broke into the walk-in refrigerators (Eric Weinberger showed me how), night and day in frantic hope, but they were empty except for milk and butter, meaning there was no purpose to break in as there was nothing to steal to eat, except for the bread and peanut butter left out for us. Once in a while a tin gallon of jam. Imagine it. Four years and almost five summers in a row with Wonderbread, butter, peanut butter and milk. Even after the first summer I was fed up, and then too, it was no use to sneak up to the farm because there was nothing there except crops, so we went to bed, drunk or sober, with our bellies empty and our eyes wild, or our eyes wild and our bellies full of Wonderbread, butter, peanut butter and milk, because there was never, never, there was *never* a morsel left over from the meals, and if we had meatloaf, cornbread, or chicken, etc., one can imagine the activity, which is why in all the documentation of the school no one has written of rats or mice — there weren't any except in certain studios, and bedrooms, as faculty members slipped a chicken leg into a paper napkin, put it in their purse or pocket, and later that night enjoyed a little snack with some wine, before retiring. That's the faculty for you.

In July of 1952 Jack Tworkov, his wife Wally and their two daughters, Hermine (around 11), and Helen (around nine), came to the school for a month. Franz Kline was due in August. So one evening in the middle of July we had pork chops for supper. I need not describe the astonishment, and anticipation as we made our way down the road, the scent of chops in the air...*chops!* But two separate events coincided to make an already astonishing event (chops for supper), much much more astonishing. I wrote this memoir in two sections, as we shall see. But that July night in 1952 was my beginning, and the two events that happened were — 1: Helen Tworkov told her sister Hermine that she Helen would be late for supper, and would Hermine save something for her. Both girls having been at the school not three weeks knew The Rule, but not in the way we did. They knew it was wrong to do it, wrong anywhere, but they didn't know the details of Black Mountain wrongness, i.e., the plate on the shelf above the stove, *food.*

2: Meanwhile, with no one knowing, except she and he, Connie Olson told Charles that she and their baby daughter Kate were going to be late for supper, and would he put aside a chop for Kate?

He did, but Hermine, who by bad luck arrived a trifle late herself, while able to have a serving for herself, yet saw there was nothing to put aside for her sister, so went into the kitchen to try and find something, and seeing the plate on the shelf above the stove, went to it, took the top plate (upside down) off, looked in, and there was a chop!

She took the chop, returned to the table and joined her family as Helen came in, and the Tworkovs as well as everyone else, save one, enjoyed a fine meal on the screened-in porch overlooking the lake, with the beautiful mountains beyond in the usual happy

Summer Session supper chatter when Connie came onto the porch with Kate on her hip, both unnoticed, and Connie whispered something into Charles' ear, and if I didn't see that I still can, but we all saw Charles rise, and in one motion swept Kate from Connie's grasp, stand up, and with the baby girl sitting in the palm of his right hand he raised his arm straight up — that child was nearly eleven feet off the floor and near enough to the rafters to make anybody dizzy as Olson let out an Ahab, Pequod, Moby Dick and Melville-shattering bellow WHO HAD STOLEN HIS DAUGHTER'S PORK CHOP? to a porchfull of people as silent as a tomb.

"Listen Fee," Hermine confided to me, seven years later in Provincetown — *"You can't tell anybody, he'll hear it, he'll still be angry. I know he will! Please!"* she laughed, trembling.

I didn't. I mean I didn't say — but I have a memory that in conversation concerning someone who had been at Black Mountain, that it was Olson himself, when I saw him in Buffalo around 1963, who said something to me about my not knowing something I should know regarding something close to school or to Olson in that sense that Olson had of things being special to him, and my trying to grasp it, and as it came clear my saying That's true! I didn't know that! but — I added, with a sly member-of-Olson's-circle smile — I know who stole Kate's pork chop.

I have here a follow-up memory, or a sudden suggestive image, knowing him as I did, seeing his face before me, I didn't tell him who, but did tell him I couldn't tell him, and I see his eyes become cold in anger, and his face set, eleven years after the fact, fifteen years after *that* fact, he looks at me in anger.

I saw him two days before he died. Pitiful.

Dan Rice had visited that day, too, as had Connie and Kate, whom Dan and me left to go to a bar. Memory says I didn't mention the pork chop incident, but knowing myself as I do, I have a hunch I told Dan. It, in the dreadful sentimental language used by certain columnists, didn't seem to matter. Wrong again.

I saw Connie and Kate on East 72nd Street about four years ago (1974), which was a surprise indeed, and in conversation I told them, hoping they'd enjoy it. They didn't.

Wrong again.

2.

But there is, or was — no, is, more to that pork chop incident than I thought, or could ever imagine, which raises an interesting question, the answer to which we'll never know because neither Charles or Connie are here to tell us, so we have at best to guess. But the question is a good one, I think. Good enough, in fact, to serve as an answer. Supposition like gossip may serve us better than the actual truths which cause both, and can give more color in the bargain.

A few weeks ago, right out of the blue I asked a friend if she had heard about the pork chop incident at Black Mountain, and because she had read my books — *The Black Mountain Book* and the Kline memoir — as well as a few vignettes I'd published after both books went out of print, she knew my work and said no, she hadn't heard of it, or read it, and as I thought I'd written it I became puzzled — I have a good memory of what I've written, and though I admit my memory can falter in terms of what I wrote, I do remember that I wrote it, so after having given the matter much thought, and getting nowhere, I realized I must have told it to someone in the way I'd one day write it, so I decided to write Olson's archivist George Butterick and ask him if he had read it somewhere. I felt strange, asking that question. How in the world could I have forgotten it? That I had omitted dance, photography, sculpture, weaving, etc., was hapless enough, plus omitting the persons involved — people were hurt and angered that I didn't even mention them in my books...but *the pork chop incident?* Which so revealed — thus I wrote George, and he replied in a letter dated 16 February, 1978, no, he hadn't read it, but had written of it in his

Guide to Maximus (University of California Press), due to be published this year, I believe, so feeling stranger than ever, with George having written his version of the incident and myself not having written mine, I realized I'd better get to work, so I went to my typewriter and wrote it — my version — in a sweat still, of not having written it, and still unhappy about what and who I'd omitted, I was therefore, in that state which writers understand: thanking God I could write it, and with luck get it in print, and — further — happy at last to tell a story the whole school witnessed, so we all could smile in the memory. Many of my books were so personal, if not private — there are passages involving other incidents that many at the school or in New York didn't experience, and in both these books' admitted subjectivity, I did omit student and faculty names and activities in favor of getting and giving the essential feel of the school and the city and my relationship to key persons involved in those locations, and vice versa. So it felt good to write something, in this new sense, for everyone.

I gave it a quick (too quick) rewrite, xeroxed it, and sent it off to George with a note that I looked forward to his response, and not a week later George wrote back:

"Oh my gosh! my gosh! We got two different stories going on here! Two different cuts of pork chops! I thought you meant the Dahlberg story, which everyone who knows Olson has heard about. I'll enclose what the hell I was talking about..."

Which he did, and I have before me pageproofs #298–300 from George's book, which gives, in fair length, the background of the early Dahlberg/Olson relationship, and in brief — around 1940 Olson and Dahlberg were both in Gloucester, both hard at work and shared meals together.

Sixteen years later (June, 1968), after the incident at Black Mountain and twenty-eight years after the one in Gloucester, in conversation, Olson (George implies) gave a mere mention to his, Olson's, Mother giving Olson (in 1940), a plate piled with fried chicken, and giving Dahlberg a leftover pork chop, which, George goes on to document, infuriated Dahlberg, who not long after, wrote Olson that in effect he Olson had bad — if any — manners, but as Dahlberg wouldn't write a sentence like that, or this, we read Dahlberg as Dahlberg loved to be read — the way he loved to write — and even if we don't read him, or can't, his letters are pure Dahlberg, and being so give cause to laughter, but it wasn't funny to Dahlberg, and in a letter to John Cech, dated 27 January, *1972,* Dahlberg again makes reference to that meal in 1940, in Gloucester. Get it?

Okay, but hidden in here is one of those little not-so-little things tied up so neat and tight even the most astute discernment might miss it, because, questions being what they are, can be raised from matters considered closed. Why, for example, in conversation in 1968 did Olson give mere mention of the 1940 Dahlberg experience, and not the one in 1952 at Black Mountain? And why was Olson, in 1968, as George writes — "apparently oblivious to the slight" — he'd given to Dahlberg? The answer to that one is Olson was like that. He hurt more characters (including Paul Goodman), in this way, than Dahlberg.

But as to his omitting the Black Mountain incident, while speculations appear to be many and varied, in a certain sense, the way it stands is the way it was, no matter the right and the wrong of it.

Olson told me in person in 1959 — in Gloucester — that he was altogether finished with Black Mountain. He was through, finished — sick of it, and perhaps sick from it.

In the early sixties at Buffalo he was more than finished (this is common knowledge). He wouldn't speak of the school, he almost didn't talk to me at all, and he never mentioned those we had both loved. It was clear he was closing the door. When I wrote him postcards his answers were curt, so I got the message, and didn't write him. Which means, or appears to mean, that in or around 1968 he'd negated the Black Mountain 1952 pork chop incident, although he remembered the 1940 Dahlberg scene. Towards the end of the sixties Olson was well aware where he stood in the world, as he was interested in the direction his thinking was taking him, and not prone to such a small incident, in particular as it wasn't so small and his rage was so big, but then — it's happened often before, to many men and women. Being drawn to his own as well as his civilization's early antecedents, it's characteristic that rascals his age will overlook what they consider only a certain period, however crucial and famous, that forms the middle stage of their lives. Olson knew what a metaphor was, just as he knew his process of selection — which, as he wrote, he served alone.

True scholarship involves the inspection of microcosmic events as well as the other kind. In this case the microcosmic touches emotions Olson wanted left alone for the rest of his life — with real reason.

Connie, however the light eater she was at meals, and in spite of her smallness (to his six feet seven), was the second most important person in his life. The ideal in Jungian therapy had enhanced the myth. He talked with her of his work, in long long conversations involving proper nouns, names, places they'd been. He depended on her. She was the second person but the first constant inspirational figure to his work, she was of his response and resource to him. His anchor and his vitality, and because he was constant in his work she had the task of being constant with him, not an easy task to comprehend much less perform.

Therefore the politician, the genius, the bluff deepfeeling yet often cruel, rule-making, overbearing Poet-Scholar and amusing man that he was, in conversation in 1968 would leave out the Black Mountain 1952 incident because that pork chop meant Connie, it meant his daughter Kate, and in recall it again meant his taking leave of Connie and Kate to go with Betty and son Charles Peter, and then — Betty's death. Olson would never mention the 1952 incident. For the associations stated above *(Maximus* is a masterpiece of associative scholarship), which must have flashed through his life again and again at the mention of a word, and the women's names in particular. His fantastic memory would leap open, and there she would be, and again, again and again — would it *ever* end? — there she was. They had shared so much, God how she

CONNIE & CHARLES OLSON

had responded! Olson himself must have gone through a disillusionment, but in any event he began to close the door to his past. And from there, in a certain conjectural view, his story became the sad story of a great, brilliant, creative poet and thinker trying to build anew from his own ruins. The dream, or wish of her revealed in the April, 1969, Andrew Leinoff interview, when Olson did a final turnabout and called Black Mountain *she** and in his secret self knew he would fail because the door he'd closed was the door to himself. This is the *Lapis,* the inner magic of *Maximus,* that allowed him to close the school and go his way, and perhaps why, through whatever mix of anger, guilt and secret suffering when he knew he was going to die, he didn't leave a will to his daughter or to his son, nor to take any steps to make their identities legal — he had never married Connie or Betty — so the children have nothing of him or from him except their memories and the majesty of his poems in print, because his estate and his archives have been bound by sale and law to other hands. I can't forgive Olson this, because he knew. If he could handle the endless legal problems of the closing of Black Mountain, he could have called a lawyer to his bedside, and in a matter of minutes make sure his children got their due. A last will is the simplest of all forms.

Wait — I'm wrong! This is what happened — I sent what I considered the final draft to the editor of this magazine [Chicago Review] about a month ago, as well as sending the aforementioned George a copy, so today, Tuesday October 17th, [1979] I received a letter from George giving, as I had requested (I felt very uneasy about Olson's not having left a will — very uneasy indeed), and George came through with blue ribbon information, as well as suggestions. I quote —

"Olson in fact left a will — naming both his children as heirs to his estate. It was just never proved, i.e. accepted by the court as legal, and so

---

*See issue number 8 of *OLSON, A Journal of the Charles Olson Archives,* beginning on page 66. For those in the know, an eye-opener if there ever was one.

disallowed in the settling of the estate. Further, the estate was finally settled, after nearly seven years of doubt and entanglement, with Charles Peter being named sole heir and beneficiary — because Kate" (became) "adopted (against her father's wishes, and, I am told, without his knowledge — so that Olson died believing she was still his daughter, i.e. in name)."

Okay, thank God I again have the chance to correct myself, and get the truth into print — some of it anyway. It's a complicated truth, and needs a little endemic detail.

I wouldn't have written what I did (of the will), unless I knew it to be true. Nobody ever told me different! But I'm leaving in my error here as a sort of warning by example. The legal news that Olson wasn't married to Connie or Betty, came late in my life, and hit with considerable shock. Just as the news, in error, of his not having left a will. In tone they overlap. I didn't understand it in the sense that I was, when I discovered it — he wasn't married — and am to this day, amazed in my particular concerned reasoning of my love for both women, and that each had a child by him. In that sense I wrote what I did.

I resented him for other reasons too, he in fact resented me and — that's a different memory, but it involves his rejection of my Kline Memoir. Olson did his best to turn the city as well as the University of Buffalo against me, and I was hurt and infuriated. I had written that book as he had hammered at me at Black Mountain. I wrote it from my roots, as he had, on a postcard written to me, around 1951 — shake 'em, and sixteen years later he wrote me ordering me to never use his name in print again — my Kline Memoir had humiliated him. Today, over ten years later, I understand why — he had changed — but in 1968 I felt betrayed, double-crossed, and in the face of his distant wrath, helpless, and after having spent several stunned days, wrote him a brief note telling him if he couldn't accept my love then he couldn't accept me. Checkmate apparent: he didn't answer. I know that the tone of my reaction is still fresh (Olson was good at that), and is evident in this memoir.

That night at school in July, 1952, following the pork chop incident at supper, when Charles and Connie were alone in their apartment in South Lodge, with perhaps a good deal of irate aftermath humor — he as well as she could keep a straight face while laughing — I can see them both, looking at each other, she knew the Dahlberg variation in 1940, you bet she did, and they must have exchanged merriment in the thought — it typifies Olson's thinking — because of that Goddamned impractical food honor system at Black Mountain, Dahlberg had gotten his revenge, and though it had taken twelve years, the amusement was on their faces, Olson still angry, and in a laugh breathing *that son of a bitch*. See the last line (in *Maximus*), of Letter 16.

The answer to the other question, why Olson was offhand in his slighting of Dahlberg is clear because it was always clear because Olson was Olson and Dahlberg was Dahlberg. Any fool could see it. But then, George quotes Olson's Mother calling Charles her "growing boy," so it can be suggested Dahlberg was a bit jealous? and piqued, as well as angry at the one chop, because in 1940 Olson was either thirty or a few months behind it, and a bit more than a growing boy, but Mother, with her humor, likes her big son to eat big no matter his age — or hers — which is true, although it can be considered in a different light, that he didn't get to be six feet seven because of heredity, apples, lentils, and salad alone. She had formed him from the beginning, a reality Connie and Betty dealt with until he had to fend for himself, and couldn't, so went to Connecticut, and Charles Boer.

Several years ago Guy Davenport wrote asking if I knew who Fernand was, in Olson's *The Kingfishers*. I didn't, then, but rereading Guy's excellent essay today I found a marginal note I'd made — "Fernand Olson's intuitive Neruda." The vowels sound, look and speak with a certain similarity. Fer, Ner, ruda, nand. Besides, it would be typical of Olson. He liked mysteries.

He wrote a novel when he was twelve, concerning the Tokyo earthquake, and at Black Mountain laughed at my shocked expression — *"You* wrote *prose?"* I gasped. Years later in Provincetown he read Raymond Chandler, said, "This guy's a real *writer!"* Olson stole food and beer from Franz Kline's refrigerator (in Provincetown), and some years beyond, in conversation at a bar in Buffalo, scorned Chandler. "I can't read those guys anymore."

I met Olson at school, in July of 1949, and four years later, in July of 1953, he sat on the dining hall steps and watched me walk down the road on my way to Saint Louis to be drafted. I don't enjoy that memory, he was indifferent, I was scared out of my wits. We'd been very close, four years in a row.

He was unpredictable in that his pattern of change was beyond his ken to the degree that he celebrated it, and I suspect at bottom he knew he was a divided man, thus change was his rule because change (which characterizes divided people, me included), was inevitable, and that being the case he willed himself to acceptance. The legendary opening line of *The Kingfishers* (Davenport: "A translation of Heraclitus's Fragment 23"), has remained vivid to me for Olson's use of the slashmark, as well as the obvious message:

What does not change / is the will to change.

I didn't know it in 1951 when I first read it, but from the several engravings in my memory, that central slashmark, with a space on either side of it, with seventeen letters to the left to form four words separated by three spaces, and seventeen letters to the right, to form five words separated by four spaces, creates oblique perfection made even more so by his syllabic structure, tone, and vision — Davenport's translation of Fragment 23: "Change alone is unchanging." — to which Olson gave monosyllabic space and breath, yet that slashmark holds a secret separation, from which distinctions may be made.

It's still in vogue, always will be, to celebrate Olson's body size, but in October of 1959 when I visited him in Gloucester, he and Betty, and infant Charles Peter, Olson and I went out to a bar, he confessed fear because he had trouble in bars: "Those little guys want to fight me." At school he and farmer Doyle Jones had a blood hatred for each other: Doyle, a short, leathery little man hated Olson out of mind; I saw them pass in the hallway that led from the kitchen to the back door of the dining hall; words (animal) were exchanged; I followed Olson outside as he strode, mind just able to control body, electrified with rage, and with nowhere to go sat on the steps of North Lodge. Dan Rice was there, Olson on the very brink opened and closed empty hands (around Doyle's neck), body shuddered, voice broke, snarled *"I can't FIGHT that little bastard!"*

Thomas Wolfe also knew.

These things of scale are in Olson's work, as well. In just about every way he was not an ordinary man, in fact he was extraordinary. But ah, how he envied, and in secret yearned to be as other men, to be a man among men. He liked tradesmen, enjoyed their company, but he could never stop learning. He was, as Jonathan said, an optimistic man, he knew great expectations, and how sensitive he could be, react as he said like a girl, and as I type I see him embarrassed, but catching himself before a blush. You can be literal about this: standing on the road by the lake clasped his hands down to bent-in knees, raised his head, aw, shit, laughed in a rush, wide-eyed (remember Olson wide-eyed?) breathed words as no one else — "A girl, a Goddamned girl!" Might it not have been true what some of us did gave stasis to his freedom to write that mystery? He gave me personal double-looks, as if to say, or to ask — *What is it? Tell me.* He *loved* a mystery, who is Fernand, a figure of voice

...already sliding along the wall of the night, losing himself in some crack of the ruins. That it should have been he —

There it is. The romantic voice, the voice of the lisping prophet who speaks (with an exclamation point), the title of the poem. It was in Olson's character as well as his work, that he was drawn to what he didn't know, an impressionistic and metaphorical labyrinth of what he did and even didn't, could and couldn't, but might figure out. In the very end, body gone, eyes in space, fingertips yet moved, trying to unravel what was yet to be found.

What we will never know, but though his eyes were "open to everything" (Davenport), those who knew him best, watched or in turn saw him as blind, he did shall I say not use the brains God gave him, but this is personal, so I'll say from it all, there is a quality or character in his work as a whole, as in certain passages, where so much is omitted he seemed to halt, select a preference, then continue. *Maximus* can be regarded as a complete (as we know it) work across an abyss of omission. *Maximus* is in real part autobiographical, so too his masterpiece *The Librarian* which seems to belong to *Maximus,* ends —

>...Where
>is Bristow? when does 1-A
>get me home? I am caught
>
>in Gloucester (What's buried
>behind Lufkin's
>Diner? Who is
>
>Frank Moore?

In the logic of the hidden, to be kept hidden, and to complete his poem, Olson — after saying (a synonym might be trapped), "caught in Gloucester" (pun on fishing in Gloucester) asks, "What's buried — " when he could have asked who, but he knew who, sure he did, because he could not have not known, but he didn't want to know, his faster than lightning mind sure knew Frank Moore, so do I, do you? the guy who made a pass at Connie, which completed the poem and left out the answer by asking an angry question. Caught in Gloucester, his whole history as well as himself, not too farfetched for a claustrophobic mind to select that burial site, and as he regarded the reader in an inclusive sense, it was typical of Olson not to hand over information anybody with wits can already see.

One doesn't have to have known him to see these things.

End August, 1950, Tim LaFarge and I stayed two days in Olson's house in Washington, D.C. He and Connie had gone to visit someone? Can't recall. But it was a beautiful, magic little house. Little. A high brick wall with vines and morning glories ran parallel with the sidewalk. In the wall, I think a small iron gate, beyond which, to the left, an untended garden grown wild. At the end of a (was it flagstone, or brick?) path, the house. Low, one storey, brick with casement windows with small panes had an effect of stained glass. The front door was inset, dark wood, with a small window covered by an iron grating. Inside the door, a small, dark hallway, wide, dark floorboards, casement windows on the left, beamed ceiling and on the righthand wall, the framed painting, a labyrinth, by Cagli. Ahead, at the end, three steps up, the little bathroom on the left, kitchen on an angle to the right, and on a sharp right turn, the livingroom-bedroom. White walls, dark wood floor, beamed ceiling, casement windows above a chest high bookcase (outside, the tangled front yard). The walls were lined with books among which I browsed, found the edition of *Finnegans Wake* his classmates at Harvard had signed and given him. All in all a scholar's library. The bed low in the extreme righthand corner, top blanket covered, memory hints, with a handwoven earth colored shawl. Bed made, stayed made. Tim and I slept in sleeping bags on the floor of the front hall. Or maybe on folded blankets and a sheet each. Every inch of the place was bewitching, and though it wasn't the slate roof seemed of straw, and we, interlopers in our Master's handmade little palace.

Across from the bed, on an angle to face it, the small messy fireplace in the left center wall (to make a five-walled room), on the mantlepiece of which the small, what, 12" x 16"? watercolor by Lawrence of a naked man, Lawrence, taking a leak in a flower bed. Beside it, in a strewn arrangement were long sticks used in the construction of rifle emplacements Olson had found on the Gettysburg battlefield. And small stone Mayan figures, smuggled out of Yucatan, for he had to have them, and at school when he'd returned, and showed them to us, as he held each figure in hand, and spoke as we watched, all in awe, he more so, Connie said she had feared every day he went to the sites, across fields of poisonous snakes. But Olson came home, home free. They stopped by school on their way to Washington. In Washington, in his little house, Tim and I held the figures in our hands and saw Olson. To the immediate left of the fireplace was a bookcase built to accommodate magazines, which I leafed through, wondering why in the world he'd read *Harper's Bazaar* until I found his beautiful poem of the drowned sailor! I'd heard him read it at school, as I type this I hear him breathe Dance boy

Dance —
Pacific Lament.

The kitchen was small as was everything in it, sink with, was there a drainboard? Small refrigerator. Small table, two chairs by a wall of windows with an inset door which opened into a greenhouse. Therefore, the house was in fact a brick cottage for him or her who tended the (long untended) greenhouse. I should perhaps check with George (there is but the one George), but memory says the reason why the yard and greenhouse had gone wild, and to seed, was because they weren't sure how long they would be there and, also, to bring it all into shape, as Connie said, would be a terrific effort. Too much. And again, notice from my description of the house, maybe a faulty memory, but I recall no desk where he wrote, and I have a nagging thread that says he wrote at the little table in the kitchen. There were a few years, before they made the full move to North Carolina, which seem transient, and in retrospect give an added dimension to their being so happy at school.

But if the house in D.C. was a magic puzzle, its most amazing feature was the stairs into the basement. Their bed abutted against a low wooden housing that sheltered the stairs, and the door to them was on the exact right of the doorway into the room, and unless you knew, you wouldn't know it was the door to the stairs, which opened outward against the doorjamb, and was no larger than three by four feet, maybe smaller, I had to bend, it was tricky for me, for Tim too, because he was taller, and as we both descended the stairs, narrow stairs, we shared real merriment in the thought of Olson, on those stairs, but for sure he had been, and would indeed be, for the shower was in the basement. Thus we took showers. Tim first, then me, laughing as we did so, to be in Olson's house with a shower in the basement and not to take a shower in Olson's shower was unthinkable. The shower had no curtain, drain at the feet — the floor was cement — and, as the ceiling was normal, but low to Olson, it was fine for us, and clear he had to bend, and twist, to wash and rinse, and if that is an image, next door, beyond the gone garden and continuing high brick wall, was the brick side of a massive five story warehouse, but there weren't any floors, and as seen through rows of open windows, from the floor to the roof in the entire building, scaffolding, where a sculptor was making the famous statue of the Marines raising the flag at Iwo Jima, their huge helmets larger than the windows, right there, next door! that sculpted monster next to Olson's little brick cottage where *he,* the Cyclops dwelt, called himself that at school, with the Greek ks, signed postcards lower case, yrs, kk. Postmarked Washington, D.C. 11 pm Jan 29 (?) 1950, on a card (1¢) typed sideways to make it diamond-shaped:

> fee:
> thanks!
> (& right you are
> saroyan is different

> — he has a little some-
> thing, no question)
>
> 2 homers for ya:
>
> THESE DAYS
>
> whatever you have to say, leave
> the roots on, let them
> dangle
>
> And the dirt
> > Just to make clear
> > where they come from
>
> THE DAY'S ORDERS, BOYS
>
> See that you keep yr passion dry
>
> And yr gun up
>
> And fire only
> when you see the light
> in an eye
>
> > love
> > kk

He enjoyed unpretentious language involving the details of labor, he had ideals about labor, as throughout his work are puns on and usage of everyday speech. He felt Pound was right in urging that Homer be brought into common language, told us in commuting from D.C. he and Connie stopped at truckstops for coffee, and listened, as he loved to do, to the drivers, Connie smiled, eager in their recent memory, enjoyed his pleasure —

"Those guys!" he breathed.

In their big rigs.

But his intensity and vision separated him from other men, from the people, in favor of preferred metaphors. All his work is permeated with his love and near fascination for history imbued with metaphorical men, women, the androgynous, his hatred of false drama involved a real rejection of realism, here he gets complex, for his awareness of the cause, he seems a paradox, but so be it, for no matter, ahead he went. To gain his ends he stopped at nothing, and his giant stride created vast omissions. Right there in those poems. But oh what he achieved! The illusion that rises off the page, in the early and middle poems, hold the expanse and daring of first individual's flight into space, those *images!* He took, as Davenport knows, his own scale in his hands and encompassed the earth. I first read his *Satyr* poem in *The Evergreen Review* and when next I saw him said the leader's woman

> A dazzling blond, the new dye making her hair a delicious streaked ash

was (in tone and context as well as image), Chandler's woman, a truth he acknowledged, and enjoyed. He liked us when we said things like that. He said he wasn't Greek ("hath not th' advantage. And of course, no Roman." I'm not sure of my punctuation, this is from memory.), but that's his sense of fun, for he went to Harvard; he was therefore of the elite. For an elite joke. Yet, in another way, the way of his body, he was, as the poems tell us.

He wanted to be used the way he liked — with advance warning. He wanted what he wanted in the way he wanted. I bet his mom spoiled him.

He was a linear man in space to his heels who would not separate a line drive from a line of verse. Yet in his magic, and there is so much, he would grasp Davenport's perception ("The national hunch," in Guy's essay caused me the most delightful laughter, and I had daydreams of the title of his 40 essays). Olson could not fail to, for so much of Davenport's work dovetails in and out of Olson's. No doubt a fine essay, for someone to write, but here it might be said that Olson's draw to what he didn't know involved shifts in himself — in a sense Olson, as he wrote, yet extended himself beyond his limitations which gives that much more credence to his statement of working within them. Keep in mind it's every word and syllable with Olson, which he followed almost beyond their meaning. How American! Davenport caught that, yet shy to extend himself outward into it, was maybe wise, while limiting himself, Davenport gave himself his full latitudes of response to perception. But Olson, who through Cagli perceived Europe and in antiquity the labyrinth, also comprehended, as we know, the Orient, and in a direct line Kline, Pollock (we were disappointed when Pollock didn't come, that summer), Charlie Parker, Miles Davis (the jazz festival fell through), Raymond Chandler's mythic woman, *The Lady from Shanghai*, that great movie, thus made connections and created an intuitive mystery beyond himself, in the face of which Davenport, standing tall, averts his own face. This is Davenport's declared difference, and limitation, from which distinctions may be made.

Tim and I had shopped at a neighborhood market, so were able to eat at Olson's, which we did, but my memory fades in these details save our bafflement in washing dishes and silverware in such small space, it seemed everything should have its place, yet where was a mystery. Anyway, Olson and Connie returned, and he said we had to go, as in okay, get out, and on that morning of our exit, the words were delivered as we woke, in fact they came in while we slept — on the floor in the front hall, with Cagli for company — memory dims, I recall sitting up, facing the interior of the house, saw the door of the bathroom open, out stepped Olson, naked, hairy, very large and *very* small, to stand on the landing three steps up, the kitchen on an angle behind him, he gazed down at us, informed us we had to go, he grinned, eyes bright at our awe, we blushed and laughed, he disappeared into the room next to the kitchen, we rose to fold sheets and blankets, and pack our things. Tim headed home to New England, I stayed in D.C. to at last find a place with Ken and Neil Noland, where I did what I'd come to do: checked in my portable typewriter at the Library of Congress, was given a small room by a large window, where for a few hours each day, five days a week for over two weeks, I typed mythology from the source text, W.H.I. Bleek's *Bushmen Tales,* of little people in the Kalahari Desert, whom at the turn of the Century, a few years after the book was published, the Dutch wiped out — the last of the pure blood Bushmen, to finish that last first race forever.

THE ROSE OF THE WORLD
ON A BASEBALL SCORECARD

Everything Olson touched revealed him, and in reading and rereading anew, his secret, confessional poem *The Rose of The World* (written Nov. 20th, 1965, and published by Andrew Crozier in England, a year after Olson died, through Andrew's *The Ferry Press*. A handsome poster in an edition of 100 copies), which at once, in a single motion went into his past and future, to remind us of the Moibus Strip which so involved him in the late Forties, keeping him ever in motion, the migrant he was, writing to cover his tracks while dazzling us with reports of his journey.

The essential key to all there is of Olson, including his personality is *The Post Office, A Memoir of His Father* (Grey Fox Press, 1975), which includes *Stocking Cap*, and a brief — very revealing — memoir of a friend of the family: *Mr. Meyer*.

This publication, along with the entire body of Olson's work, is enough to give in fair detail all one would want to know, of the character of this great poet, and misunderstood man. This is the seminal work.

The other work, as close as a work by another person can be to the poet himself, is Charles Boer's *Charles Olson in Connecticut* (Swallow Press, 1975). The extended quotations — on the spot stuff — of Olson, plus Boer's integrity, memory, incredible scholarship, having studied with Olson in Buffalo, can not only keep up with Olson's almost Labyrinthine voyages in history, but offer fresh sources AND AT LAST be *severe* in his criticism (calling Olson, along with Norman Mailer and Louis Armstrong, a big baby), but retain his awe, and empathy, in a love I share, for Olson. It is so *good!* Aspects that need not be explained, for example throughout, between the lines, is Olson's certainty he's going to die, soon, and has come to visit the author, in Connecticut, to beg a resting place, on the last mile of his migration. The symbolic impact of this book matches its subject, such as none other to date and, by the way things look, none other shall.

So there is one seminal work, with its companion volume. Tie both in with the fact that Olson's mother, who was quite a small woman, spoiled him. Without her he never would have made it as far. She gave him license, go all the way.

She, therefore, is his seminal woman, not, by the way, uncommon, in the arts. Not a lot needs to be known about her, assumptions can be made, but she is his matrix, and in his difficult relations with his father, stood by the boy, and — it reads no other way — protected him, saving the day but little knowing her doomsday punch, in terms of his relations with other men *and* women. Throughout *Post Office* hidden references of antagonism towards Olson Senior who, preoccupied in work or getting away from things, didn't affect his son the way, or to the degree, his son wanted, and was unable to demand. A favorite film of Olson's was *Red River*. The father/son in their sexual fistfights. John Wayne. Montgomery Clift. And with his explosive feelings, it didn't take much to cause flare-ups.

In 1934 his father due to go to a National Convention for Mail Carriers, in Cleveland. Olson Sr. had long prepared for this trip, as it was complex and political in many ways, his fight back from the way they'd treated him. And on the night before he left, asked his son if he could borrow his suitcase which was "bigger and newer than his." But Olson — around twenty-four — says he needed it himself (without saying why), and refuses. His father went away angry, and in a passage of the worst writing I have ever read by an adult it reads that in a relative sense soon after Olson's father was hospitalized and in August of the next year (1935) died. Heart. But on his son's every visit, no matter how long the boy stayed his father would neither speak to him nor acknowledge his presence.

Remember Olson broken-hearted in Spoleto in the 60s. Pound, who refused to speak to him?

In 1948, in writing *Post Office*, says, "...it is only now that I realize at no time did he admit a notice of me. Or do I exaggerate and punish myself anew for the guilt of my refusal of the suitcase. I do not know."

In the sense that having made no effort at a direct vision or comprehension of his emotions, and — common — turning to magic, left himself more vulnerable to any event beyond his control, meaning he would never understand or experience the fact of change, or renewal.

On receiving the news of Betty's death, in the auto accident, Olson fainted. Four short years later he was dying.

And glancing through *Olson in Connecticut*, gazing into its prisms, I unrolled my copy of *The Rose of The World*, and read it again. Olson's poem of Olson's fate: synopsis of The Master. His metaphor for his guilt, preferred I should say, the rose, whose petals and thorns, conceal, deep in its center so true to his style of secrecy: *the suitcase.*

He had stepped behind walls in his youth, to be unseen, in a secret (insecure and obvious) boy's life, which created a brilliant, political diplomat in maturity, later at the side of The President of The United States. But as big as he was, six feet seven, beside F.D.R. in the white House, he was never as big as his father, no boy ever is.

Stocking Cap tells a hidden story he wouldn't dare — his ultra awareness of his father, his own constant vulnerability, caused a later Olson, in reaction, to redefine the universe, the origins, patterns and destiny of all humankind, by going as Pound said, "out the back door of Greece," into prehistory, where Olson could come to his own conclusions, as he stood up to face — and articulate and record — the sum total of *all* history as far as he could see, in his kind of poetry.

This is what happens to genius, entangled with parent. See Mozart. But a little self-knowledge might have — ah yes, so indeed it might have, but it didn't. So his followers will never know how unhappy he was. The magic was running out. Make no mistake. He knew it.

The Rose of The World is his hidden suitcase, his true metaphor. *And,* in re language, his use of the word "thing" stands as revelation! It was hot, it seethed, as if long repressed, but in his hand came alive, a living organ? His own? *Could be.* All through his life the phrase "the odd thing about it was," or "this most curious thing," emerged from a yesteryear literature of radio and Victorian intrigue, that mystified him, and in his genius, throughout his life, in every instance his use of the word, see "thing" as *Dark Spirit,* or *The Unmentionable* or *handle/suitcase.*

This is why — one reason — he was so controlled and formal, because language was beyond his control. He used words without knowing what they meant. He told me. At school.

He had heard 19th Century adjectives — odd, curious, queer — as a little boy, and his impressionistic, genius ear linked them to the word "thing" before he scarce knew what it was (and it never was what it was), from the beginning it held a mystery he couldn't grasp — a great source for metaphors — and in part explains his sentimentality which he despised: controlled with an iron will. But movies were his undoing.

The one with Jimmy Stewart, where he falls in love with the beautiful Indian girl, who gets killed at the end and Olson almost *died,* and instead of admitting it, and like Philip Guston, who said he wept at those awful Irish (priest/cop/poor kids) movies (I said I wept at movies, too), and we laughed, standing at the bar together, Philip and I laughing, how *good* that felt! Olson *never* admitted it, even the night Mary accused him, point blank, of being sentimental. He almost blushed, flustered, didn't know what to do. We laughed, embarrassed.

These little things, long blocked, build into greedy tumors. These little things *all* relate. These little things are the family within. For another instance of Olson making much of nothing, again refusing to admit, see p. 20 bottom, top p. 21, *Olson in Connecticut.* Laughter and amusement at one's own silliness was not one of

Olson's features. His rejection of false drama was — is more viable today than ever, for its use in an increasing totalitarian world. But his hidden hatred of it has its roots, in part concerning his father's clowning, which near humiliated Olson, who used the word "antics" *(Post Office)*.

Connie in reaction to him, might yet have let him know, on their arrival home after the movie, and they might have shared a smile, he no doubt happy, so I may be wrong. But she would have let him know by diplomacy...

Yet when the film came out, it had a certain impact — story of interracial love — and whoever the actress was, she was very beautiful indeed, in her Indian-appearing pancaked skin (was its name *Straight Arrow?)* — anyway, she knocked Olson for a loop. It could be that the man he was and the poet too, in a sense had never together cut loose, even in his youth, so not long after seeing the movie, the aspect of seeing the young piano student, Betty Kaiser, at school, might well have stirred him deep, in particular if she made first moves toward him.

Where threads cross over, in the weave of character, the story gets good.

At lunch one day, on the porch, sitting across a table from him, for an unrecalled reason we were talking about movies, and I said, no doubt wild-eyed, and ecstatic to be able to say one thing I could at last say with conviction, *"The Lady from Shanghai!"* Olson almost choked. His eyes got wide — all at once, snap! jaw dropped, blurted: *"You too?"*

Important to a study of his life, would be that film, starring (and directed by) Orson Welles, with his then wife Rita Hayworth. Her hair was cut and dyed platinum, filmed in black and white with such skill it's recalled in color. And but for the scene in the judge's chamber, where Welles knocks things around, it's a great movie, working on the same premise that Raymond Chandler used: the beautiful woman as unrepentant killer, which Chandler took from Hammett (Maltese Falcon), but as all good, and creative thieves (like Olson), he made into his own, by giving detailed focus to the woman (*The Long Goodbye* comes to mind), and giving her an allure no writer has before or since, not even Maugham, who made here and there, a try.

At the end of the film, she is dying, and begs Welles not to leave her, but he does, in a stunning vista of high-angle camera with his voice-over, still leaves me breathless.

But the word 'leave' is the word, so here we are again, departing. Page 34 bottom *(Post Office)* Olson's father had planned ahead, which "was not like him. *I take that from him.* (my italics) He much preferred to set off, recklessly sure that things would work out in their courses…"

So the very lush, gorgeous, just plain *beautiful* Rita Hayworth begs him not to leave but he does, not in truth because she would have killed him, tossed the gun in the bay and herself departed, whistling. But because it was over, which indeed it was. But, as with Chandler's leading women, the hidden and always unsaid fact was they were real only in the eyes of the men who saw them, and, in particular the detective, Marlowe. Chandler made them rich so they didn't do anything, but be rich, and bored. They never worked, or had thoughts, did the dishes, or read a book.

They were in truth unreal, and their unreal story was over and again one of beguilement toward death, she lured men to their destruction. *The Long Goodbye* is a very very good novel, and its aura of characterization, down to the houseboy Candy, is astonishing.

We know Olson read, and liked Chandler, a lot. And I know that Olson had quit reading "that stuff" with a shrug, but as well as I remember him telling me, I remember sensing or being aware of something else. Olson had gone into *Maximus* and in part said so long to the world, but I had the feeling, with his one more farewell, that he was a little too cavalier on that one, as if taking leave of an essential part of his character, but on the other hand, it could well be, it sure fits his pattern, yet all the same, it's difficult, in particular if you've never known it, if you've never been bad, but wanted to, as all men want it, to be beguiled by a beautiful woman. It has a lot to do with self-hatred and self-destruction, and a lot to do with mother and incest, it has a lot to do with doing the forbidden, and for certain men at crossroads, a lot to do with growing up, by seeing what it is, to be lured, tempted, to yearn, to die for her, to be with her, lose yourself in her, and to laze around after, a while, and play her game. He hated not knowing and he didn't know. But...who is to say? He put it behind him, yes. They might say. Until Betty showed up, and let him know, and that Soviet airship in his dream dropped a bomb that blasted his life.

The celluloid image, by the way, is an aspect of his anima. She is passion and danger. She stands on the road to maturity, she is right out of Homer, and baby, she can sing, just as she did in the movie, on the yacht, remember? In her swimsuit, platinum blonde, on her back, gazing up at the camera: *Please don't love me...*

I say "an aspect" of his anima. There was another woman who I know nothing about, but Tom Clark does, and will give detail to, in his biography of Olson. She was real. Olson knew her in the 1940s. In his notes is his realization that she was his anima, but with a difference: she was his intellectual equal, or so he regarded her.

His lifelong usage in writing, and in speaking in expression of awe, which in his presence was impressive and spooky, like mature people recalling dramatic situations use with deep emphasis words from early childhood. And with the feel for language like he had, way back, his encounter with his father, the suitcase, his father's silence and death electrified, transfigured him, in guilt, that for the rest of his life hit him hard — *hard* hard — by way of sudden, unexpected dreadful news to which he was always vulnerable: in the most raw way. In part he died, with Betty.

He was one of the few characters around *not* in the Pandora syndrome. Not a matter what was in the suitcase, it was the very *image* of it, its life and death potential in being what it was, and why he was right to stress image and right again in saying in class "Why make a simile if you can make a metaphor." The backlash, from being the migrant he was made the metaphor — so explosive a possibility, to use it made it the same size as he was, so potent and obsessive he created a personal art form and language to confront it.

Everything he did reflected everything of his involvement. In this he was in constant completion, yet appearing to leave so much undone. Another deception. Perhaps enigma. Arriving at Black Mountain in his way, lest he forget D.C., but leaving D.C. to remember it, to leave in the unsure conviction of return, vowing never. All touches everything. He arrived to stay with Boer end September 1969, died 90 plus days later. He had showed up, to meet Boer, empty-handed. No valise, no "thing." Boer soon realized it was not the stated visit. See page 32. Just amazing.

Olson sent this scorecard to me at school. Envelope postmarked June 3rd, 1950. Washington, D.C. He'd been to the ballpark and seen a game between the St. Louis Browns — my team — and the Washington Senators.

Notice that the long curved line down the center of the card doesn't meet the top of the other line. Scorecards in those days were printed on cheap cardboard, and sold folded in half. So Olson wrote my last name first, having Ostrowski in mind — Senators' left fielder — was not going to let fielder get confused with Fielding: make distinct the proper from the common noun, and wrote my name that way, curving an ink line out and in, and all around to YR BOYS, curving another line, like the curve of a cheek, toward the bottom of the top half of the card, flipped it over, and continued down to DID ALL RIGHT! 5–4, 12 innings, with a long lateral curving line toward a drawn ¾ circle, with tiny words inside, regarding Ostrowski, and the Senators' second baseman, Michaels.

But in the way of all of his work, this is perhaps another one of his messages that, given slight changes in visual word arrangement, related to and might predict *The Rose of The World*.

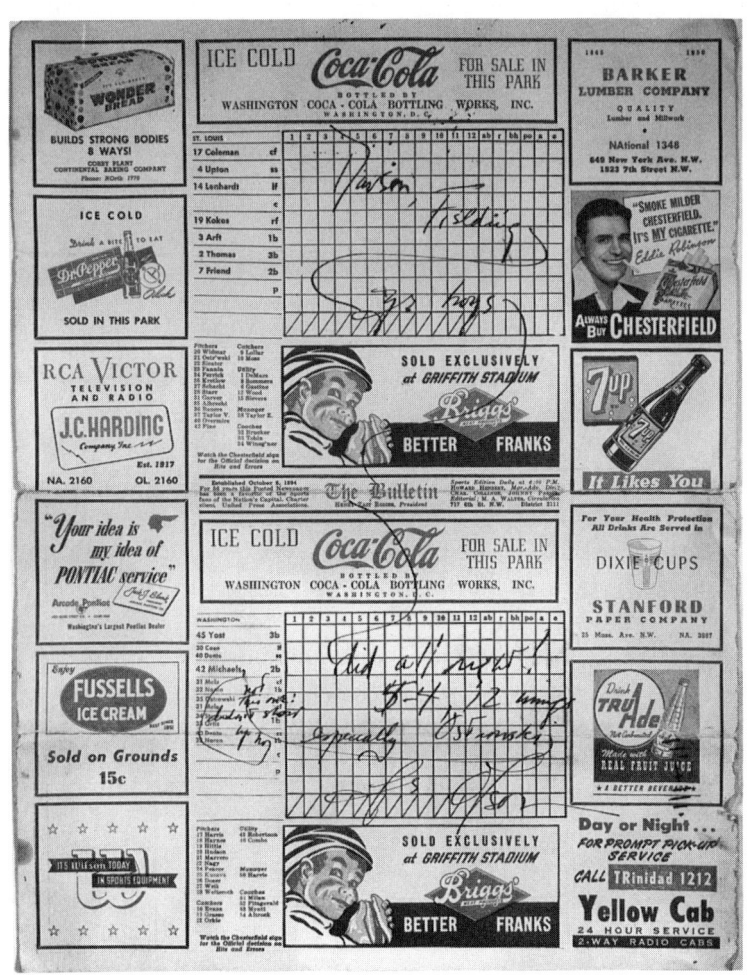

BASEBALL SCORECARD

THE ROSE OF THE WORLD

BY CHARLES OLSON

BETTY KAISER

MY DEAR MRS. DAWSON:

                          Black Mt
                          Feb 28 52

My dear Mrs Dawson: You must forgive me I have not written you sooner. But I have been locked in a couple of long prose go's, and they have a way of blotting out any responsibility but themselves.

    For what I had to report to you was the most delightful biz., the meeting of the Faculty in which Fee, (in the regular process of all the students one by one being considered as to how their courses were going, their work, and their general state) — in which Fee was enthusiastically praised by *every* single member. It was a sort of triumph — and Dr Dehn in particular, the classic sort of Heidelberg professor, spoke out of the contrast of Fee as citizen now to all previous states of him! The rest of us, who were in course with him, marked the swift advance of him — and I was gratified to hear the others, like Fiore, speak of him as I spoke to you of that sudden rise of his acuity in December.

    It is all splendid, & does, I think (you will have been aware of the show he had of his new paintings, & how very much he has made his own base, is painting & writing from a confidence of position which he has hewn out for himself, a use of *actuality* which is very fresh and, in that show, stood out here where such a move as his is not usual

                                                    — a

taking up from the rhythms of what he *sees*

                        Well, the point is, without any direct monkeying with that that troubled you & Cara in the Christmas time, at present Fee is SOLID, is HIMSELF, and is working without, so far as I can see, any but the healthiest influences — and those essentially both here, and out there where Melville are, where Shahn is (where Goozer was) — where you are.

Clearly, Mrs Dawson, he's in the clear, and you & Cara can put the whole business out of your minds. And though it seems damn pat — seems what I predicted — I am saying it on the basis of the evidence *since* Xmas.

He's very beautiful the way he is facing to everything — like a *man,* like they say.

And if he had come to me with a course card showing DANCE, I'd have said, yes, I would have approved — for yr nervousness over that, in yr note to Mr. Huss, was quite unnecessary. As you probably know, he is so busy with French, painting, & writing he chose not to make any such departure. But my point is, he is so straight and on the ball that *anything* he chooses to do is coming out the straight end.

OK? Believe me.

Cordially,

Olson

AT THE FARM

THE SERIES WAS OVER. The Yankees beat the Dodgers. It began to rain and Terry came across the field till he got to where I was standing. He said it's raining and I said, Yes, it's raining but I was thinking what Joe would say at supper. I was laughing to myself about Cleveland. I told Terry the Yanks won and he said Oh really? and I said yes and he didn't care because I was thinking they won The Series: The Yanks Have Won The Series like in a story the name the title but like it was them winning The Series in headline I could smell that paper and he said as he held out his hand with his palm up he said it's raining but doesn't it smell nice and I grinned and said Yes and then he asked me what we should be doing and I pointed at the rows of plowed up potatoes and said

We should be picking those up.
With what?
Our hands.
Where do they go?
In baskets.
Baskets? Where are they?
At the end of the field. I pointed. Over there. He got some. I saw Jones drive the tractor into the shed. I thought he looked like Floyd, a little, but different because Floyd looks more loose on the tractor and comfortable. Don came walking out and went to bring the cows down to be milked.

Some of the potatoes are little, some are big, they grow in clumps and like Terry said you can walk ten feet and not find a potato and then find a dozen. It was not him who said that it was Dan. Terry picked up a basket and so did I and we began at one end of the row and we picked up potatoes and put the full baskets up by the road so they could be picked up with the truck and then we began with new baskets on a new row and we got them filled too, and Terry asked me what to do next and I said,

Now we rake.

What is that?

At the end of the row there's a potato fork and you get that. There's one missing. I'll get another at the barn, Dole said there's one around somewhere. You rake at the side of the furrow, you just rake the loose dirt, break up the clumps and look for potatoes. It's not hard but it's something.

Okay.

I'll go and try and find the fork now. You go ahead. I'll get back soon.

He went to the end of the row to get the fork that was lying there and I went to the other end of the field to the barn awhile and couldn't find it so I went down the road and turned by the fence by the ditch and I looked under Dole's house and then, by the trees, I saw a long handle. It wasn't a fork it was a hoe and I thought that I would use that as well so I took that and cut across the field from the house to where Terry was standing raking and he was doing it all wrong so I showed him how to do it and he said,

Oh yes, that's a good way, too.

It began to let up a little but then rained harder. Terry said that it was raining harder than before and I said, Yes, it is. Dole came down the road in his Ford and turned into the yard in front of his house and he stopped. He got out and came to where we were working and asked me if I found the rake.

No, I said.

Terry said it was raining.

It sure is, Dole said. He looked at me.

Ain't it. I said,

It sure is. Dole said,

How much you done?

About two and a half rows.

That's good. Tomorrow we'll bring in some tobacco.

Then he went across the field to the house and Terry and I watched him. I said that it must be near six and Terry said he didn't know and I said, Well, when we finish this row, we'll quit and he didn't say anything. He began raking potatoes and I did too and a little while later we put the hoe and fork under the house and walked down to supper and he asked if this kind of weather keeps up for long down here and I said it sure does. You get used to it. It stays like this and when it's different it's snow and gets colder and after that it gets windy and blows out doors and windows. After that it gets hot and then like this again. He frowned and said Jesus. He was from Boston.

THE NEXT DAY

The next day it was raining again and Floyd jumped up on the tractor and yelled TOOT TOOT and the tractor began to move ahead, Dole and I stood on the wagon in back. It was loaded with tobacco. Dole and I laughed and so did Cleary's father and Dan. Terry walked up ahead to pull the threaded tobacco stakes up to put on the wagon to take to the barn where we would hang them and wait until it stopped raining. When the tobacco was cut the stalks were pushed over the gav which is a metal tip on the end of a stake, and when there are five or seven or eight stalks, the stake is pulled up, loaded on the wagon and taken to be hung in the barn to dry and later the shriveled leaves are taken off the stakes and graded. But the tobacco barn wasn't finished yet and Dole was hanging the stakes full of tobacco in the cow barn, the beef stall and in the barn where I saw Buck given an injection for his bad eye. Floyd held Buck's head and they tied a rope around his neck and brought it around a beam and held the end of the rope and Floyd said, Buck's a good bull.

The wagon jerked a little from side to side as it went through the mud. Up ahead Dan and Cleary's father had a stake ready for us when the wagon slid to a stop. Floyd and Dan shouted at the tractor because it was still skidding on even after Floyd stopped it. But finally it stopped and Dan and Cleary's father handed the stake up to us and Dole told Cleary's father to be careful and Cleary's father sort of smiled, we took the stake with all the tobacco leaves threaded on it and we laid it very carefully like a tablecloth over the other stakes of leaves and we did it very carefully, not to injure the leaves. Then Terry gave us a stake and then Cleary's father and then Dan and then Terry again and Floyd got off the tractor and helped and so on until the wagon was piled high and we went to the barn. We sat in the doorway of the barn and looked out at the rain and big dark clouds hanging over the mountains that surrounded the valley. Dole said that turkeys are crazy. They follow you around and get in your way because they walk around in the rain. I could see Floyd looking out from the doorway across fields and he said to Dole,

You got company, Dole.

A car came skittering up the road pretty fast and slid into the yard in front of the house. I wondered if Cleary was there, the man was knocking on the door and then he quit and got in his car and we watched him back out and turn and drive up to the barn and stop in front of us. He got out and came toward us and nobody said anything. Then he said he was looking for the man that ran the farm for the College and Dole said,

That's me.

Floyd said at the same time, pointing at Dole, He's right there. Dole and the man talked a little, after the man introduced himself, about some custom work that he had to have done would Dole send somebody down sometime soon. Dole said that he would and smiled at Dan. Dan here would be down Tuesday morning. Then they squatted down on their haunches in the doorway of the barn and one of the turkeys got up and walked around on the hood of that man's car and Dole went over and it flew off and we laughed and Dole said they were ignorant things they always got in your way. Dole and the man talked about plowing and how hard plowing had been a few months before because of the drought and I watched the man roll a cigarette. He had blonde hair and a white shirt. Floyd was inside the barn tapping his hand on one of the steel bars that separated the cow stalls. He was back in the corner and I wondered if Floyd knew the blonde man. Floyd was all loose, tapping his hand on the steel bar waiting for Dole to stop.

The sun came out and the chickens and turkeys and guineas and bantys were walking around and Floyd rattled a chain on the bar and Dole said that field out there had been hard when they had plowed it and he asked Dan if he wasn't right and Dan said yet that was right and after the man had gone and when the tobacco had been put in and we were finishing up cutting corn and the sun was shining bright and the shadows were long across the floor of the valley I asked Floyd if he knew that man and he said no that he didn't know him, I don't know many people around here, I come from California. I thought of that bent license plate on his old Dodge as I looked at him and Floyd said he sure thought that man talked a lot.

MORE NOTES FROM OLSON'S CLASSES

Eckerman's conversations with Goethe — Everyman

A fact of our life means nothing insofar as it is truth, only insofar as it is consequence.
      Goethe

"You essentially *eat* your way through your own medium."

History — the way it is presented — is a fraud, because it diminishes the act of our own touching of the past.

Elizabethan secular world & secular vision — sense of life — see use of...(unclear) — gold, etc., secular plus — profane divine — motion — assuming God is motion

Milton to Melville & Goethe is boring (concept of Devil) Boring to Jews (conception of God)

Scientific prose in 19th Cent is best.

Whole modern concept of education is 18th Cent.

Metaphor nothing to do with comparison — it's recognition

Metaphor is *not* what a thing is *like:* it's how it behaves!

like a coin with a head on one side and a merry-go-round on the other

Wherever you can avoid a qualification, leave it out — however — it being — seeming.

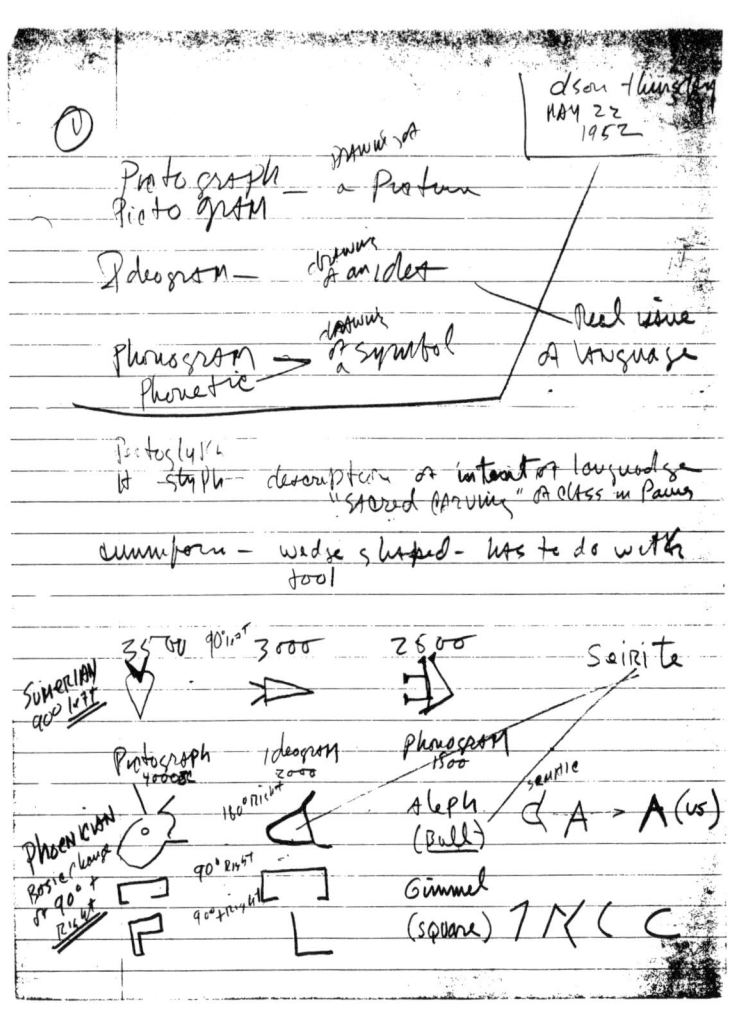

F.D.'S NOTES FROM OLSON'S CLASS

VICTOR KALOS

TO THE
MOTHER OF THE PITCHER

                    Black Mt. College   Black Mt   NC
                              March 11 52
To the mother of the pitcher:
                as the mother of such a son, i am not surprised that you have done this real wild thing — pointed, with yr bat at my center-field wall, saying, I'm sending you a present, and — it must be only this once in my life that anything came smashing HOME!
              i'm am so delighted that i have to put it this way so that you'll guess, it isn't just pleasure, but it's the BELL!
                                        you hit me, — right on the BUTTON!
                      Can't believe it. Can't honestly think *anything* could hit as this wondrous bone hits, this SCRIMSHAW!
                                            WOW
    I sd to Con, when she told me the pacage was over there, what do you think it is? I sd. Whldn't it be wonderful if it were a carved ship in a bottle? And again, you beat it, this TOOTH is — for a man like me — BEYOND any such didling as a carved ship in a bottle: that is, this is *straight* skill, not ingenuity, fussing with the act. This is a man putting his hand to a surface — a given, seized surface — and WORKING it, head on (hand(on
              And let me tell you another thing: as I was admiring it for the severalth time yesterday after it came in, I got a stir: I got the damndest feeling. For you see, the most prized thing we brought back from the Yucatan was also a BONE! A remarkable thing: the

carved thigh bone of a man — with a fine Mayan human figure, & a long fine hieroglyph passage. It has become a sort of fetish to me of my long lifed drive down & back of the American thing as we've had it — and NOW, you add for me another fetish, what feels to me like its complement, the fetish of my own direct tradition: those latter day guys i went to sea with as a kid, New England houses, say, that stem of mine, Mr. Herman Melville, this thing, a whale, and men's hands — what they'll find time to do.

               I am immensely pleasured, and when that is true I always drift imagistically toward what the good people call superstition.

               You've given me MAGIC, Mrs Dawson: how about that?

               (Also, this secret: for the yrs that i did study such matters, I also studied scrimshaw, in the hands of friends, and, of course, in the museums. AND I WANTED ONE. And never, of course, had one. AND NOW I HAVE, with uttermost thanks to you.

         No, you couldn't have bettered it, not at all!
         My deepest yrs
         Charles Olson

ELLEN SCHASBERGER

YOU BELONG TO ME

Sitting with Don Jones at a table by the front window in Peek's Tavern, and if you don't believe me, you *ask* him. Listening to the jukebox I'll never quite know why but it has something to do with The Second World War. Far away places. Hearing it again just a few days ago this September month, 1989, Don Jones sat across from me and we drank Budweiser, it was a good beer then, and we almost wept from the song. Her last chorus, jungles wet *with rain*, what the great torch singers of the 30s and 40s had done, she made slick and neat but it worked, and still works today,

> Fly the ocean
> in a silver plane
> see the jungle
> when it's wet
>   with rain

That's what got us.
Got me. Gets me.
I see the plane, a DC-3, over the Pacific, and Don Jones and me, near tears in Ma Peek's Tavern while Jo Stafford sings her commercial heart out.

THE FINGER

The person who got the worst raw deal was John McCandless, the printer. Maybe he shouldn't have been there — at least during the Olson years — as the good students we were, should from his point of view have gathered round him, at least offered the respect he felt was his due, and he was right.

But the changes the school went through were violent, and not kind. I don't understand the power play that went on (nor in truth do I want to), but we were beyond the Steinbeck and the novelists of that period McCandless was interested in — he led a class on the novel, using those books — because our focus was on poetics rather than plot development, toward the development of a new style, as well as a new mode of delivery. I was doing full figure ink drawings lifesize — six feet or more — close likenesses in sixty seconds or less, Nick had written a Noh play for himself and Victor, which was staged. Joe made the facemasks. Olson was beginning to change how the poetic line would appear on the page, in a historical statement and dimension. All history. Any statement, anyone interested in a new style: write your own poem.

With memory as source, without fear of association or of self-consciousness. Take it through the mountain, not over. (Rimbaud)

John McCandless was the printer, and a Quaker. Bob and Sue Turner, whom I visited a couple years ago, in Alfred, New York… remembered John. He had been a Conscientious Objector during World War II — not a mere non-combatant medic (like me ten years later), but a real C.O. Those men had guts, taking a stance like that, in *that* war, where *everybody* wanted to kill. And he should have been treated with respect, but he wasn't. He was a good man. I liked him. He taught me how to set type, by hand, and to print —

I'd learned at home but John taught me so I could do it on my own — those little pamphlets I did there, of my own poems, in 1950 and '51, that sell for over a hundred dollars each, were done in that little print shop, and as I write, I'm standing beside John McCandless, tall, too thin man (angry and anxious about being ignored), and we gaze along the reverse side of the page, looking for too deep an impression, from the bite of the small rows of 10 point Futura, locked into their frame, in the handpress.

Couple years later.

John Chamberlain used that print shop for his early steel sculptures, telling me that late at night, in that deep, Carolina darkness, his welding torch caused Olson to exclaim from the road, some distance away, to the bluewhite flashes through the trees —
"The finger of God touches Black Mountain!"

WHERE ELSE?

Certain people — a lot more than you'd think — kept an eye on Black Mountain, because that's where what was new was going on. Also true about the schools that evolved from it — Goddard, Reed, Bard, Antioch, Cranbrook, etc., — not many — so regarded. But Black Mountain was the real vanguard.

Where else was a composer playing music on the inside of a piano, a dancer knowing the members of his troupe by their footfall, or artists stretching — and exhibiting — blank canvases? Where else could you sit on top of a mountain and look down through clouds at the school you attended?

MY APOLOGIES

Nights it was too much, all too much, we went a little crazy.

The waterfight. Chasing each other through the Studies Building late one night, with pump waterfilled fire extinguishers, not many of us three, four? Drenched, and wild. Kicked in Harvey's door, there he was, reading, sitting beside his stereo system, listening to a Beethoven Quartet. I asked him to come out and he said no so I let him have it. Soaked everything. Books, papers, records, moving turntable, and him as he sat there, aw Harvey, why didn't you get to your feet and kick my ass out?

Last heard he's in Southern California with a bunch of kids and I hope a happy wife. Would love to see him. Look in his eyes. Say hi. Give him a hug.

WOW

Sitting with others on the steps to North Lodge he kissed me, a French kiss, mind you: deep and long in his passion, and conquest: a professional from the big leagues, *in the big town.*
   HERE!
I retreated into a former personality.

SUMMER OF '48

Ray Spillenger — Tuesday, July 10, in conversation said he had graduated from Pratt in 1948 and, seeing the little ad in *The Nation*, that Mark Tobey would be teaching at Black Mountain that summer, decided to go down. So, he took the train, we agreed it was a beautiful ride, and the closer it got, people got off until there was no one in the car Ray was in, except himself and two fellas in the back.

Rose from his seat, went back to them. Introductions —

John Cage, Merce Cunningham. Ray said he was going to study with Mark Tobey, no, Cage said, he's sick, another artist is taking his place. Who is that? Ray asked. DeKooning. Cage knew DeKooning. Ray had heard of DeKooning. So typical of the school's hiring policies. I discovered Pat Passloff was there, too, that summer, where she and Ray and Bill (DeK) became such close friends.

I should check this with Joe, but Ray also said that was the summer Joe Fiore decided to continue studies as an artist, rather than musician. His dad, violinist for the Cleveland Orchestra under George Szell...Joe talked with Bill...

A play by Satie produced. Ray and Bill with others worked on the sets — details available elsewhere — and because there were no curtains because it was done in the Dining Hall, newspapers were placed over the stage objects, and just before action began, newspapers whisked away. Albers, who sat beside Ray in the audience — keep in mind Albers' interest in textural collage (cardboard egg crates, etc) — said to Ray, that he liked it better with the newspapers.

Ray leaned close, telling me. In his kitchen, as I sipped Scotch and water over ice, Ray cried — and I agreed. I knew.

"He was right! It *did* look better!"

Adding, in his hallway before I left, that stage set Bill made would go for a million.

Said Peter Grippe was there that summer, and I recalled meeting him, in the Fifties, at the Cedar? But Pat Passloff remains a mystery to me. Always liked her, and her work. I have the feeling she's a source person, so far untapped. With an original, or only touched-on point of view, still but in regards to Milton Resnick. But that she was at school that summer, and met Ray and Bill, gives the matter an added dimension.

SUMMER OF '51

Rauschenberg and Twombly on the gravel patio beneath the Studies Building, gazing down at a large canvas, covered in most part by tar. They tossed handfuls of pebbles on it. Motherwell, between them, gestured. Said to throw more, and they did.
 "More."
 They did.
 "More."
 They did.

Bob and Cy posed for a couple of drawing classes. Nude. The model didn't show up. They rose from their drawing boards, walked to the front, and began to strip.

CY TWOMBLY
*(F.D., 1957, Casein on Butcher Paper,
Photograph by Mimi Fronczak)*

THE FISHQUEEN

There was and is an aspect of me that enjoys being vulgar and funky, and on those long, dull nights with no money, nothing to drink, no food, it was as if the earth rose up, folded us down into itself, and we shed our manners, our frills and culture, and became...different.

There was a student whose name I won't mention, but he was slender, tall and blonde. From the south. Was wicked, and funny.

I see the long, dim corridor of the Studies Building. It is late, and bored out of our minds we sit outside my study, on the floor, leaning against the walls, in the dead of night as he pleads to a young lady student from New York we know is a Lesbian. His hands are out, fingers spread, why? Why would she not let him lick her pussy? He didn't want to fuck her, he just wanted to —

"Did you ask her?"

"Yay-us Ah asked her."

"What did she say?"

"She called me a Goddamn fishqueen!"

We laughed.

I had never thought of it before, nor had I heard the word, but they both sounded wonderful. I knew her, by way of a kind of worship of the unattainable, to be with her was a thrill, and a mystery, so I wouldn't think to ask her, but that night he gave me the idea, it appealed to me. I liked it. I liked thinking about it, and was amused.

But I never asked her. Never. Not because it was so vulgar, but because she would say no, and realize who I had been talking to — that fishqueen — and I would change (for the worse) in her eyes, which he would think was funny — she would too (with her little smile), in her crisp shirts, as I sat at my desk in my study, looking at my typewriter, very near death because I *couldn't* write it, I *didn't* know, even as the world spun outside my window, even as I heard a voice, ever patient,

But you will.
You will know.

I leaned forward, folded my arms over my portable, lowered my head, and in the buzz of a thousand insects, closed my eyes.

MOVIE STARS

One day in the late 60s, during the cocktail hour at Max's Kansas City, standing at the bar with Mike Schapiro (our third baseman on Max's softball team), I noticed a few feet away, a very tall, older gentleman looking on with others at a large poster — gallery announcement — of a nude, stretched across the hood of a car, and I said, to Mike, look at that dirty old man eatin' up that photo.

"Know who that dirty old man is?" he asked.

No.

"The Raggedy Man, in *The Red Badge of Courage*." Pause. "John Dierkes."

John Dierkes!

I crossed the floor, and stood beside him, noticing how striking he was, with so much obvious character, I said excuse me and he turned.

"Yes?" smiling down, bushy eyebrows raised.

"Do you know the poet Charles Olson?"

Big smile, deep, warm eyes,

"One of my dearest friends."

We shook hands as I introduced myself. Saying Olson had been my teacher at Black Mountain. Which began a friendship that lasted until John returned to the west coast, and some years later, in conversation, his name came up, and Barbara Rice mentioned he had died. Near Topanga, where she and Jack live.

I feel a little guilty, in thinking of John, because I was so self-involved, unhappy and anxious, in a separation with my wife. I was in therapy, and rather living that experience, far removed from this elder gentleman, who in that sense was conservative, yet working for UNESCO, and privy to interesting information.

He had known Olson during the FDR administration, and on direct appointment from FDR was in charge of all Negro troops in England, during WWII… Dierkes very proud of that, and in talking about England, London, where he was stationed, with his friend Edward R. Murrow, with whom he sat during Murrow's overseas broadcasts. Imagine my thrill, to meet a man who sat beside the man to whom I listened, with millions of others, enthralled as bombs fell on distant London, and Big Ben began to toll the hour, that voice of voices: *"Good evening. This is Edward R. Murrow from London…"*

Dierkes' description of both of them, one night — broadcasting locations shifted — on steps leading down to a cellar flooded with water, amid coils of electric cables rigged up by CBS (CBS had meaning in those days), and Murrow talked, with his magic, melodramatic, patient voice as the water rose, higher and higher…

Dierkes being patient with my questions, but understood what that voice meant to me—us, each evening at home, the later you-are-there voice but we weren't there, we were far away, but not so far as we would be were we without it, for his voice was the connection that kept us suspended and gave to that war its melodramatic — fractured, fragmented—sense of distance, which Hiroshima dissolved, and television and advertising have transformed into emptiness. We at home, listening to Murrow, heard in his voice the beginning of a calculated distillation of the past and future into the present, where we have remained, oblivious, since. Without the horizon inherent in distance from the Renaissance on, or the sense of space as savages knew until the white man appeared: space, vast field of freedom, and energy. Gone. Another meaning of The Second World War.

Dierkes was in *Shane*. He's the guy that falls off the balcony into the haywagon — very proud of that, no stuntman for him! Towards the end of the film, in the shootout. He was also in *Jubal*, remember that one? With Glenn Ford, and Ernest Borgnine? There's a scene in the corral of a close-up of Dierkes that's priceless. His tall figure, large, broad, craggy face, deepset eyes...with another actor whose name I can't remember, but today quite famous. In context, a couple of cowhands, expressionless in a corral, leaning against a split rail fence. Mountains in the background...

At school, with Olson in the lead, we were ardent fans of Chaplin. Victor, who, if he wished, could be as funny as anyone, in one of his rare adventures in ambition, wanted to meet and if possible study with Chaplin, to my dismay: what would Black Mountain be without Victor? It would continue to be, but not the same. So, on Olson's encouragement, Victor went to Hollywood, Olson having told him go see John Dierkes, he'll tell you how to get to Chaplin, and it all came true, except that Chaplin had left America to never return, and Victor came back to school.

Having lunch with Dierkes in a luncheonette on Third Avenue and 17th Street, middle aged waitress paused, looking at him, recognition dawning —
"Haven't I seen you on tv?"
"Yes." Smile.
She glanced at me, my grin, before saying how nice, and taking our order.
So, I thought. That's how it's done.
And writing this, I recall he had a part in a movie that was in production, and I asked if I could come and watch, to which he said no, he had to have total silence in utter privacy: nobody there but director and crew. But he again understood my enthusiasm.
This must have been in the late spring of 1968, because he said the word was at UNESCO that, in his second term, Bobby Kennedy was going to tax the corporations.

In the same spirit Olson sent Victor to Hollywood, Olson wanted to make a movie, a western, on location at Black Mountain. His attention on the American west gave him the idea, so he sat up all night and who knows how long into the next day writing a *long* letter to John Wayne, outlining ideas for the movie, reasons for doing it, maybe lending detail to the part he imagined that actor would play.

But why write an actor? Why didn't he write John Huston, with whom he'd worked as advisor on the first *Moby Dick,* the one that failed? Or, why didn't he call up Dierkes? There was a pay phone outside the Office — we didn't have telephones where we lived. There was also a pay phone inside the front door of the Studies Building. Call and ask Dierkes' advice, who should Olson go to. Or ask for Huston's phone number, or address? What else could Olson expect to receive as answer to his letter but an autographed 8½ x 11" glossy of John Wayne, that the studio sent?

P.S.

He wrote Einstein saying he needed a statement on Black Mountain, and Einstein delivered, remember?
    Carve *that* in stone, I say. Black Mountain failed?
    Only to the failures did it fail, and to not even all of them, in truth, such was its success.

THE EINSTEIN LETTER

January 16, 1954

To whom it may concern!

    I have followed since years with a vivid interest the development of Black Mountain College. The reason for this interest is that I am convinced that education without a vivid personal relationship between all working together there, students as well as teachers, is far from the ideal even if the teachers are of highest standing. The University has not only to transmit knowledge from one generation to the other but is also a place where characters and social coherence have to be developed.

    It is, in my opinion, of great importance that those smaller institutions of learning, so beneficial to the development of harmonious personalities, are favored in every possible way. We have to prevent that mass-production is extended to human beings themselves.

Albert Einstein.

FIRE, AND AFTERMATH

The woodframed, brownshingled house where Wes and Bea and Joe and Mary (upstairs) lived, burned, and they lost everything. Everything. In the beginning, for it went fast, Joe ran upstairs to try to save what he could—a fine record collection...but he fainted on the steps. Basil, who had been in London during the Blitz, ran in and brought him out, saving his life. I hated Basil for that, of course I was proud of him. We all were, dashing forward to help out...clever of me to hate him, while despising, loathing myself. Was in a mood. Not myself. Somebody else, far away, as memorable as the fire.

Next morning, Mark discovered among the ashes a copy of *Paterson*, burnt through to the passage about the fire.

Tommy Jackson's MG broke down in Virginia not long after that spring vacation, as he drove back to school, and he phoned Joe, said if Joe would come and get him, he'd build him a new turntable and cabinet. True. Joe did. And Tommy did but, as Joe was known to say, it took a while.

OUR WAY

The core fact of the school was its developed discipline toward composition. From the beginning. Community has been the tag word, and in part that was true, there were those minded people at school, but with Josef and Anni Albers, composition was what it was about. Design, too. No, not a composed community, a community that composed. More than did or *what* we did, was compose.

We were as disciplined to see as we were to draw. Drawing came from seeing. Looking came from seeing. Focus, next, followed by drawing.

Some of us drew on paper on the floor, some sat on benches and drew on drawing boards. We entered the classroom next to the weaving room (empty after Anni left), which (two rooms) formed the bottom floor of the Studies Building. We came in, got our things set up, and as the model struck a pose, we watched. We saw her, and looked at her while thinking how we were going to draw her, as we focused on her in the way she would be composed on the paper, we began to draw.

We were involved in how form appears in selections from intuitive choices that satisfy changing intuitions of balance, or center, which explains those strange-sounding words of those days, *painting blind. I can't get into it. It won't let me in.* To pass through conscious awareness to a deeper, more intuitive eye seeking a balance, a center that once was established became the chance for the beginning of each painting or drawing or potential series.

Before we made any move to actual painting — touching pencil, pen or brush to paper, we were seen in body positions of thought and focus, poised, pen or pencil inches away from the surface, hand and eye searching for the place — the appropriate unseen place to make contact. Later, not much, while helping Franz in his studio in New York, and watching him paint, it was the same. Different, but same.

What belonged where was the dominant concern, the first point of energy and focus. In its purity, it included color.

INFLUENCE: MONDRIAN. THE DRAWINGS.

Seeing, at Sidney Janis Gallery early this year, a small retrospective of Mondrian, just looking at the work, recalled Black Mountain in the most sensory, tactile way, I almost smelled it.

I knew Joe and Mary would like the show, and they did.

At my home in the midwest, in June this year, after my mother died, going through all my things by way of cleaning out the house, before it was sold, seeing the pencil studies in composition I did at school, there he was, all over again. Mondrian.

POKER

One of the studies overlooking the lake, a few doors away from mine, became our poker den, and for several months we played almost every night until quite late. In the fine histories written by folks who weren't at the school, this has not been mentioned.

Eric Weinberger, Joel Oppenheimer, Basil King, Joan Heller, Jay Watt, Danny Haugaard, Jack Boyd and myself made up the regulars, although Joan tended to fold early and away to bed. I don't recall the effect it had on our studies but what drinking cokes did to my teeth is history, and as for our studies it cannot have done us any good. The games often began a while after supper and lasted often until dawn or near enough that there wasn't much space before certain eight o'clock classes.

The poker games were often loud, the room filled with smoke and all too often nothing to drink except cokes or maybe some coffee somebody prepared on a hotplate, until Bert and Basil went into the Homebrew business. We were poor, so the winner never won very much, yet to be a winner was WONDERFUL yes, it *was* the game that was the thing but to lose was so awful, and after the money ran out we gambled our records, our books, anything, which is how I happened to buy Jay's Webster Chicago automatic record player because I had won most of his Woody Herman, Stan Kenton and other big band 78s, and needed a machine to play 'em on. My mother sent me the money and the deal was made.

He seemed to have a good hand, seven card, you know, so being broke he bet *Northwest Passage, Happiness Is A Thing Called Joe, Apple Honey,* raised with *Bijou* and went bust to all our amusement.

Jay studied music, one of Lou's students. Had once played

trombone with Claude Thornhill. His breakup with Misi was tough, but he began going with Viola Farber, a piano student who later switched to dance, under Merce, and became a member of his troupe. Couple years ago she was invited by the French Minister of Culture to be the guest director of dance for that nation. Not bad.

Jay was okay, in his way, sardonic, caustic with a horrible inward gasp-like squawk laugh others noticed and he thought was funny, in contrast to being erudite, urbane, witty, and he was.

Eric of course ever quiet and Basil never at home with wisecracks and snappy chatter, sitting beside Eric — they were very close — near Joel, who kept up the chatter as did I. Joan a quiet person. Jack Boyd who wanted to write a Broadway musical or a best selling big novel was perhaps in the wrong school, although I enjoy my memories of him, and had I been a little more erudite, urbane and witty, I would have collaborated on that musical.

Danny Haugaard was it seemed on his way somewhere, for I have no recall of him at school save around the poker table, and those two nights with Jack Boyd, two hands of poker played out such as none other. Danny won both. Jack bet everything he had and he had precious little. Played his cards well. But lost, as memory reaches back, long into the night, only the regulars at the table, as the cards dealt, bet, and in a gesture turned, I hear Jack curse, how had Danny gotten that ace? Just as we were asking, eyes wide. But a couple of weeks later, which memory says was the last game of poker that group of us played, at least in that little room.

On the last hand, that last night, Danny was given two aces, both of course face down. After five cards dealt, he had a pair of queens showing.

Jack had a pair of kings. In his hand he had a pair of tens, or jacks.

On the next to last card Jack was dealt another king, face up, so he had three kings showing. Danny was given an ace, so he had a pair of queens with an ace, showing.

Boyd was getting antsy, asking each of us around the table,

"What the fuck does he have? Why is he staying in? You know what *I've* got!"

We all nodded. It was true. He had a king high full house. We knew it.

"Maybe he has four queens," somebody said.

"No," somebody else: "I had a queen."

"Aw shut the fuck up," Joel complained. "You *ruin* the game!"

"Joel's right," Eric.

True, true, we knew.

On the last card, dealt of course face down, Jack was given a king, and Danny an ace. Tension running high, we all leaned forward, having dropped out — deferred to the sluggers — long ago, watching these guys, at it again, with dawn, and Flola's French class not far away. The room smelled like a Bowery ginmill. Jack bet everything he had knowing he had him. *Knowing* he did.

"He *can't* win. *Can't!*"

He had long fingernails. Raised a corner. Peeped.

He looked just a little bit, just a little bit, his head more narrow, longer nose, he liked to drink, W.C. Fields.

"Impossible," he said, and in the showdown, bet everything he had. Pushed it forward, into the kitty. All of it, his chips, cash, stood up, emptied his pockets, laughing.

Danny didn't do that because it was out of character, he bet all he had without drama, in his way, quiet, calm, thin smile.

He looked a lot like that movie star whose name I can never remember, who was married to Natalie Wood, and in the surprise that James Baldwin described in Richard Wright being round, having expected a squared figure, Danny (not Dan or Daniel), had that silky hair, soft pink skin and boyish aw shucks style of smile, but was large-boned, with big hands and I think feet as well as shoulders, knees and elbows, an amusing contradiction, he was fun to watch. Rather brusque, impatient? Looked at the horizon like there was something there. Had a good poker face, and as Jack turned over his three kings, Danny with a fine smile that became a broad grin, and a laugh, to our utter, and complete amazement, turned over his three aces.

Not much later Danny left for Europe...a few years later I saw Jack in New York, having a drink at Pete's on Irving Place and 18th St. He would not give up his romance with Thomas Wolfe...

I discovered by the experience of winning, in a streak of luck, what it was like, which being a small thing, one night in a school far away, it was no fun for anybody else, and it never happened again until in a transient Army scene I played poker on a blanket over a cot with guys I didn't know, and again got lucky, recognized what it was, and played my cards well until they were getting angry, and I was getting scared. I played one more hand, bet high, with violence in the air I showed my hole card, swept the money off the blanket and ran for the door, out the door, and away to the train to New York. Quite a while later, on a lecture tour, witnessed a man at a table in Vegas lose several hundred dollars, on a streak, but he didn't have the smarts, the intuition, to stop, and lost everything. Perhaps those poker games at school were a touch of the world. Maybe we stepped outside the crystal...

Joel one night said we — at the table — couldn't raise after we passed. During a game around midnight, maybe he was losing, cause enough to declare a new rule, but maybe not. Joel a stickler on this kind of detail (and from those days through the rest of my life, Joel an influence on my paying close attention to certain accumulating details in my writing such as drinking and cigarette smoking, being sure to remember, in my story, how many of both each character has had, which is why people in my writing don't drink or smoke, with rare exceptions, it's too much work. The last story I gave focus to was *The Secret Circle*. Not that it matters, but for the hell of it, while writing *and* rewriting it I felt Joel at my side, bidding me *watch those details),* for he was good at math, with a poet's ear, can't beat that. He was a sturdy guy, strong back, shoulders and legs. Played football at Cornell...but more sensitive to appearances than people believed, personality adjusting to how he thought he should be seen, heard, in an unsure way, bringing him to mistaken conclusions, and insights that in retrospect are sentimental. I think his unsureness was because he disliked or hated but anyway was never influenced by his father, thus father ineffective, causing him like a lot of men including me, to make mistakes in choice of women, and because he never did anything about being unsure, he wrote all those poems about an imagined state of being a woman and, while ignoring what it was in fact to *be* a woman, gained a good readership of fans who — innocent, like him — thought what he wrote was true. But that's not all about Joel. He was far smarter than most, because he understood pretty early on that his limitations were real, and rather than go the intuitive, creative poet-genius road, so often involving self-destruction, he like Allen Ginsberg, chose common sense, and having accepted that he couldn't drink anymore, took it in stride, and in that way, became one of those people who live day by day in a conscious maybe a little cautious, but yet alert style. He liked life, realized he was sensitive, but found strength in his awareness, and made his name out there in the arena with the best of them. Many people loved him. He was a good father, in his alert way, *he* knew what father meant, witness his sons, yet there's more to that story, too. Max Finstein, of whom no one has written, and though some years dead, deserves attention in spite of himself. Max's failure to acknowledge certain people and their circles (LeRoi Jones, who published Max's poetry). But it could be said that Max was the closest thing to a father Joel ever had, which in part explains Joel's behavior, strange as it seemed. Working a nine to five job and coming home to Max and his wife, every day. But Joel loved Max. So did I. Everybody loved Max. Who didn't? We glanced at each other.

It would have been like Eric, to ask him,
"Come again?"
"You can't raise after you pass," Joel repeated.
"Says who?" somebody said.
"Well, I mean," Joel began, gesturing, and Eric, as Basil and I smiled to each other, interrupted, stated:

"You mean we can't raise after we pass."

"That's news to me," Jack Boyd.

"I never heard it." Danny.

"Me neither." Me.

"Come on!" somebody. Jay. "Play cards!"

"Yes! Play cards!"

But Eric and Basil and Joel, being Jewish, and seated as in a row, had to have it out. And it would have been so like Eric to get it. To understand. As Joel said,

"It's been a rule as long as I've been playing, and — "

"Where was that?"

Joel put his hands in his lap, lowered his head, and began to cry. Well.

We gaped.

"In the Bronx," Joel murmured, sniffling.

"But Joel," Eric said, gentle, loving, touching Joel's shoulder, "This isn't the Bronx."

WHY BLACK MOUNTAIN WAS LIKE A PRISON

Paradise contains its opposite: prisoner in isolation far from the world.

And in character, many many inmates don't dream because prison is the bad dream they wake in every day. I have no memory of my dreams at school…afterwards, yes. By the dozens, a couple recurring, in particular of walking the short cut to the farm.

Prison too is atemporal. Clocks for the guards. Inmates have told me. It is true that in the houses of detention, city jails and medium security prisons, clocks and calendars come into focus, because these places are transient. But prisons as known — Sing Sing, San Quentin, Marion, etc., the big joints with the *high* walls — so unreal so dreamlike, inhuman, so numb, vile, *unconscious*, the guards so asleep and ignorant (precise opposite from school), chronos had (and has) no meaning. No use, no purpose. For who? Except the guards? We knew meals were served because one of the cooks came outside and raising the lead pipe, rang the iron gong — I see Cornelia doing it! We heard that echoing sound wherever we were. All we needed for structure, for we attended classes in a sustained concentration surrounded by landscape and sky: the reason why in anxiety and depression we felt trapped, it seemed so local, so claustrophobic, inescapable: *and we let each other suffer, in secret keeping watch.* I went to the doctor twice in four years. Once for poison ivy. The other was a mockery…we didn't go to doctors until death came in the gate, up the road, in a thunder of hooves, plumed black horses drawing a black carriage heading toward someone's house: Rozie, remember? Appendix burst, *just* made it to the hospital...close call! And of course the incident with the bee, and Dan.

The seasons were profound, yet subtle.

Relationships mattered in more ways than we dared admit. For far less than is admitted in prison, there is all manner of violence including murder. Some inmates do dare say it, and live to tell it but — who to? Even today, in writing this — even today!

Beginning 1967, I must yet go low key, be diplomatic. But the first rule of the memoir still holds true — it hurts that Seymour Krim's not alive to read this, who helped and encouraged as none other — the memoir reveals more its author than its subject because the subject appears through and because of the author: the memoir is the primary subjective, personal literary form, hence the value, with hyperbole and eccentricities marking its authenticity and point of view as well as charm. So. If I didn't put myself on the line, it would ring of opinion rather than of experience and history.

We were so important to each other we dared not say so. *Dared* not! There were strange developments, changes, maybe transitions, of the most intense and sustained complexities day and night in cycles where things got so intricate we could play music on it (those hollow tortoise shells and drinking glasses filled to various levels with water that Lou Harrison played with sticks like chopsticks — and students learned how to conduct. I think it symbolic of our selves,* in that valley, not to break the spell — there was no spell — so many deep and vivid connections and bonds and difficult dizzying prospects for me — because we meant more than one to each other, the way Nick meant Victor but Victor meant *Tim and Cynthia*, so it was, quite so, very possible to in passing overhear a voice from near or far — night or day — cry:

"Not *me!*"

---

*The continuous but hidden, secret, even unspoken dialogues between some persons were vivid, yet seemed to go as if ignored, which set the tone for the future (typical Black Mountain: being what it was yet will be): on my first going behind the walls in Attica — at 53! — to lead a writers workshop, I afterwards felt I had been at Black Mountain. Even today, prison classes so intense, recall the school.

And know who spoke by the tone, and through that the identity of the person they were thought to have been.... This is why the school comes under attention, or discussion in its sociology and art, to bring an understanding to it, in combinations of text and images, as to illustrate but not define. That will come only on the creation of what we were to each other: not just what we did, and the things we said. It was not family or a cohesive kind of group, but by the creative consequence of our relation to our art and imagination and experience in life — depending — to/on each other, why we were so important to each other. Nothing so characterizes prison as this because so much focus, with so much intensity, is given to *what our potential was,* or in prison is, which puts all the media, the guards, walls and gun towers in the background, which in turn is the meaning of *on the draft* — being transferred to another prison — breaking up close close friendships, and with inmates forbidden to write to each other in different prisons, inmates let the other fellows go, in a seeming cynical feeling. But what can they do? So, let it go. Let it be. There are friends I knew and loved at school who live near me and whom I never, or seldom see. It's okay.

In a passage in the first edition of this, where she (unnamed), walks outside a building into the night, I think, I (have the feeling) that I rush to the door and call after her — *I dared to:*

"I love you!"

"No!" her voice trailed back. "It's you."

"No! It's YOU!"

"No..."

I waited.

But there was silence.

Some ways back one night I visited Fredonia College, in New Hampshire, and no question about it. In its way, way out of world space, its close darkness, I felt Black Mountain's character. So too, in Arizona, that beautiful, remote high school, Verde Valley, with its more controlled, overseered type of freedom. But in those places and so few others, like at Black Mountain and inside prisons, it's the inmates who matter: among themselves how much they mean to each other but never say, because of a difficult, complex fear, pride, edgy transience, and awareness in distance of things so close, maybe too close, which fit, and belong to an unclear, unspoken vital pattern.

This, which defines a huge aspect of prison life, was the heart and soul, the pulse within the crystal: Black Mountain. In the risks we took with each other, *to dare:* stands the true experience, the accurate adventure, of the school.

WHY WE WENT THERE

Between the lines of almost everything in print on the school, was its genius to make, to transform us into more of what we could be, and in its way, by doing so reshape and define itself, as it did with Cage in his Happening, making him in altogether his way, create it.

But because of material and — important — critical reviews presented by people who didn't go to the school, we're compelled to consider Black Mountain in light of the famous names who went there, like an exotic elite with racist undertones — that kind of arrogance. How this is not true but still seems so is because of educated and artistic jealousy manipulating the media to justify any point of view based on no experience.

A similar type of person labeled the school Communist for the same reasons, confounded by the thorn of Black Mountain's persistence.

So while *The Thing* was on its way to the little movie house in the town of Black Mountain, where Victor and I would see it, and Doyle Jones talked turkey with local people about growing and harvesting and curing tobacco, and Paul and Vera Williams did what they did in Minimum House built from his design with student help — diving board matting wall to wall over a concrete floor — sliding glass doors onto a pebble terrace with a view into trees and a whole WALL of rhododendron and a creek below...

While Stefan and Hilda composed in domestic harmony, and Mrs. Jalo and Mary and Mark read *The Cantos* aloud, and checked references, Bob Turner I betcha made the plates and cups and the rest that Sue used on their table, good Quakers, good people... Hazel went on taking beautiful photos, Russell Edson — and his sister Pat in her layers of sweaters curled up on a pillow, reading

Baudelaire. Bert Morgan in his study with *The New Yorker* before going up to the farm to milk the cows, and Cornelia and Malrey in the kitchen, having a smoke and a nip of Malrey's peach brandy — homemade stuff and potent, as tall, lean Ben, the local handyman in bib overalls sat by the stoves and no doubt thought all the world mad. So.

Harvey and J.P. Grady were holed up in Harvey's room, each in his own bed surrounded by mountains of books, magazines and newspapers for weeks, even months, with a narrow footpath to the front door and bathroom (shared) and the room beyond that, where Jorge and Pat Nelson made merry whoopee, in the same room that had been Nick's: across the hall from my room, in the all wood, frame building called South Lodge, which in Carolina seasons changed smells and sensations only wood makes possible... Nick had been a student of Albers, and painted the walls of his bedroom black and the floor white. He was neat in his ways and I yet see him, in his white cotton pants and shirt of home dyed, pastel color with no collar, as if asleep, stretched out, face up on his mattress on the floor — no bedframe — sheets a little awry, in one of his trances, doing mental masturbation in which he was successful — as he had said, and I discovered true: to this day recommended, like a wet dream awake but a handsoff job guaranteed to please, although it does, like they say, take some doing.

There are places deep in daylight on the mountain and in the valley where shadows walked, trees came so close, all kinds of trees, and among them bushes seemed a state of mind, slender trunks and limbs, and clouds of little leaves. The experience of being surrounded by, to be within rhododendron is lifelong, for the color, texture and effect is as close to reverie as we can get: beckoning toward an embrace on its syllabic chanting name or a call across some mythic river by a half-naked figure, hands cupped around mouth in a call that is the expression of that fact: rho-do-dendron: leaves so green, as smooth as the bellies of frogs.

We didn't look at the landscape, for in our discipline to draw and paint, to compose and perform, to write and read, to read and think, we looked into it. Much the same way as we saw each other. With love, in friendship, and disdain or anxiety, antagonism or weariness: our awareness of each other was sustained, and at points sublime, foolish, embarrassing to be sure, who were we to say we were different from anyone else, anywhere else: at Black Mountain, all once, continuing. To say Dorothea's relationship with Esteban Vincente was one of student to teacher, and that was true indeed, but what she learned is in her work today, just as what I did is in mine. Chamberlain outspoken: ditto. Black Mountain will be to the point where it awaits discovery. In my book saying we were like snakes was true: the direct atemporal involvement within our selves, bodies, spirits was organic and free, yet it bound us through our commitment to its recognition, as a snake aware, we were creatures of our own cognizance: seeing and being were one.

Affecting everything.

The concept — tested — of sequence (first things first) changes in freedom (from that of captivity and rules, orders, bulletins…), so too that of near and far, which varied to the degree of our location and involvement.

The world around us — lake, sky, mountains — seemed closer while we were indoors, because in our awareness it followed us in. If we were outside it receded but only to a point for it was always ready to move. During meals and concerts in the Dining Hall the frogs around the lake brought the lake to our tables and chairs because we heard them. Herons and egrets, standing in the shallows near the Pot Shop, gave perspective to distance by being in the foreground of the Blue Ridge skyline, but across the lake from us. In that world, as we wrote or painted or composed, and were inside our work, unaware of anything but it, we merged or blended in and became space immersed in local, cosmic distance, as it must have been with the first peoples. Walking along the road, down a hill, in a field at the farm, just crossing a road, we went through it, and in an intuitive sense, there were almost corridors.

Bucky Fuller's constructions were at home at school for lots of reasons including their obvious looking like they didn't belong there. Stood out. But in their exaggerated spinal, spidery way, they resembled veins of leaves, even snowflakes, which is why on his construct being raised, fell flat, he was wise to credit it as lesson, not as a disaster. The pieces didn't work, the experiment continued, just as he did, having learned.

The way the school transformed us into what we further became to be, gave memory a character of prediction. By living out what we had learned, we would advance into the new feeling we'd been there before. I had had an eye on the future while standing by the lake which involved remembering I had done that, long before I had. In a way I had been prepared to go to school before I got there and I think that's true with others, too. What remained for me was to follow that same direction after I left school, to continue to change toward an intuitive future from an intuitive past, with those kind of memories, predictive in their nature, to writing this book, *and again and its rewrite,* to in large part declare that I had an understanding, that I had an intuition of the composition of things: arrangement was something I had a grip on in high school before, but which Black Mountain unfurled, in its my first real, great inspiration.

This is why I don't serve the beauty of selection alone, because I knew I would change, but where would I fit? I knew I would change, and adjust in a gradual, unexpected, surprising way that no matter how I resisted it and I did, I would know I *had* changed, because things were beginning to fit. I died a lot in those changes, in different unexpected ways of dying, and in the big ones where I was right in dying, for suffering, I understood and understand the meaning of renewal, of being reborn, and of the many mystical things in life. But still, *why* don't things work? Where do I fit? Will I? Where? And how? To many the focus on tomorrow is on an exit, not to me. The dawn is Entrance. To atemporal people the present is the moving point of transition from yesterday to tomorrow, for to atemporal people *there is no present:* and baseball is the game without clocks.

An intuitive state which the 10th Street painters understood without knowing it, on getting "inside the work" or on knowing when it's done, the painting "tells you," etc. They and we at school with them, had found a new formula for doing new work (nothing new can come any other way), and the formula fit the work. We will always need and want a new form of art that involves new ways of structuring perception and response so it will create an independent image while retaining tonal contacts with its origins, and their beginnings, like the whole process of becoming embarrassed. Obvious, any fool can see, but why? How did it happen?

Turned beet red.

What did he say?

I don't know! Look!

At Black Mountain I first became aware that I had emotional problems, clear cut, some easy to see, like being too self-conscious.

Mary said I was too giving, that I didn't know how to take. It hit home because in truth I wanted to take, or have somebody give *me* something, but not knowing how, and in fear of it — doing that "Give it to me" — which would cause horrible guilt afterwards, I continued to be too giving, and it took writing this to recall her words.

Victor saying the word "Moot." Memorable.

At lunch Jay talking to Viola in a certain tone of voice, across at her, not to her. I see her face set, eyes get bright, as she leans toward him, and speaks right back, and we laugh. How jealous I was.

For several months a student bullied me. No, say who it was. This story defines the school, and he'll recall it or — if he does or doesn't, it won't matter. Nick bullied me, so much smarter and indeed all I was not, as I loved him there and shall of course always, although he is not in this way, in this way of feeling in heart's spirit perhaps. I went into a tailspin, it went on and on until, in a bad state, I confessed to Mary and she said Nick was jealous. So it must have been clear, but not to me, and reveals my blindness to myself, but I chose my opportunity and let him have it, saying Mary had said so, which ended the matter.

What it means is I learned why he was jealous, and in truth, knowing why was one of the true reasons I had to leave Black Mountain, not all that long after he did: I knew how good I was.

Olson wrote in a letter from Yucatan — took writing this to remember — asking me to tell him more about a girl I'd written him about... *more about the girl...*

The book I would most want to write would be the one where I would be Cicely Shellhase: no one has been so every which way at once continuing.

I wish I had been more knowledgeable, more in control, with a little more confidence, so I could have known her better. I identified with her, felt so close to her, the way she behaved as if a mirror stood before me, she acted out me it seemed, more than I would ever dare. Her sensitivity, how smart and creative she was, safe, impatient, demanding in her loneliness, she knew what to say but so self-conscious and vulnerable with others she was terrified to speak, and tore her hair, happy and laughing to be able to do that, but in anguish because she had to, she didn't know what else to do to express herself, and people saw her, causing her war of feelings, each with a voice, in wild outcries, mutters, sobs, low complaints, and laughter as she sat, bent over, tortured: tossing her head, tearing her heart out.

A NEW LOOK INTO AN OLD STORY

The beginning of the decline of father in the west, and the rise of mother began with the industrial revolution because it broke tradition with home life, by getting mom out of the house, and transforming her influence from inner sanctums, to open streets and outer speech, as she began to make money on her own. The power behind the throne — which had held up the illusions of patriarchy — was gone.

Yet the illusion remained, and it seems incredible that in two whopping wars, where men on a scale unknown went into combat to die or to return injured and unfit, yet — through advertising at least (still controlled by men) — the illusions persisted with father as head of family and religion. The modernization of *The Book of Common Prayer* was an advertising trick. To prepare a text for the people to read is to prepare them for advertising, on which religion, today, is based. Thus the placing of father as head of family in religious dogma is suspect. It was assumed that mother was supposed to take care of things at home while making ends meet. This hardened her resolve, and it was clear, as she looked around at available options, that it was still going to continue, and angry at the double deal, mom said, okay, dad, you can't have the illusion of control while I do *all* the work AND nurse and raise and keep all of you healthy, give power where power is due, to your mom.

Simplified, exaggerated, but in brief true enough, and, if you can read between the lines, the diabolical and horrific stress factors involved between parents, their society and the pervasive moral standards, including the usual western traits of racism, vindictive intolerance and greed, all with no concern for the future.

The gradual or, depending on your point of view — mine, for example — rapid decline of father, heading toward a gathering zero-factor in American ghettos, bodes ill for tomorrow's mass of fatherless children, perhaps reflecting in microcosm, the fate of a handful of men and women in the U.S. in the late 1920s, through the 1930s...

In subtle ways it was happening everywhere, but because America was dedicated to only itself the things we did were obvious. Europe was more entrenched, complex, habitformed. Artists still reflected patterns and attitudes, but in the U.S., in a not yet understood reaction to war in distant lands — with WW II looming — the homefront was going through a secret, inner, combat pathology of its own, so you add The Depression and the usual things, plus the vanishing father, and rise of mom, there were also changes in the arts. Things seemed to stand out here, where in Europe they had been in a tradition of assimilation to in fact form, even support the culture.

Toward the end of the 1920s and through the 30s, a small group of artists, young men and women, from across the country made their way to either San Francisco or to New York, because of the reputations of both cities for artistic freedom and therefore acceptance, where the arts and culture thrived.

Behind the tons of available background data to support this — between the lines it was more than that, that caused their going, which was not only the displacement of leaving home for a new home, but for the young men, for many of them it was the departure from a loving, supportive, but powerful, even creative mother. It may be true with the young women, I can't say. I know it was true — father either ineffective, dead or gone, artists more sensitive, and in the arts of that period, look at the families portrayed, and the sons who lived to write the plays. The American obsession with event — the media hammers its bedlam into us every day — reveals a national insecurity over not being able to be at home because at home we're saturated with the media drowning us in event, thus the frenzy over security, and no wonder.

Pre-television, CD, VCR, MTV, even photo-offset much less Xerox process, on the verge of FM radio it was the same but not so obvious, there were a lot less people alive. If somebody's father died, somewhere, everybody knew it. If somebody's dog ran away across the valley, people were concerned. As I got on the train to go away to school, twenty-five people saw me off. Franz Kline went with his wife to New York City to be an artist, to live in Greenwich Village, and paint, of course he'd been an artist in high school everybody knew it, those cartoons in the yearbook. His father had died, early on. He was in a school for boys in Philadelphia, raised by his mother, until she married again, to his stepfather, a railroad engineer.

Look at those paintings, it's right there. All of it.

Philip Guston found his father, dead, hanging from a beam.

Pollock's father ineffective, his mother an overwhelming influence. I'll bet DeKooning same or similar in re mother, and Gorky, too. Look at the women in their works...there's more. I bet Motherwell fits in there, too. I know I do, but I didn't go to New York — I went to Black Mountain, which Franz called Downtown Manhattan, because what we were doing at school, faculty and students, paralleled the action in New York, and my fellow students, Basil and Jorge and Dan, the same thing, it could read that we had to get away from mother, to come into our own.

Even perhaps away from women — who but mother was ever less? — to explain our famous macho attitudes — taught, note, by teachers (Olson) who came from the same background — I think as men in truth we didn't know how to be, and in a childish way maybe wanted — needed — the women we wanted in the way we wanted...maybe.

But the women or girls weren't just sidekicks, they too were painters, which created potential new problems that *were* new! Not model as artist's mistress, in fact no longer mistress, but girlfriend *who also painted!*

But with the getaway from mother and the women who appeared in all art history, in painting or sculpture or song or poem, of nature or the figure of herself, with all her feminine characteristics, posed, eternal, on the pedestal, for his art. Or her art, indeed. Woman's body was *the* subject, next to nature, to work from, had been from the beginning.

So in removing art from its historical subject, and creating things few could see and understand, it would be natural to call it a name — abstract, — Expressionist, thus Abstract Expressionist, common sense for educated, erudite critics who do not paint.

But the basic dual personalities appeared and yet still do — geometric control in its varying degrees, with its famous names, just as the free-wheeling uncorkers, with their variations and their famous names.

There is a *lot* to be said because, at this point the work of each artist should be studied. Motherwell in his obvious sexual impulse work. Styll in his cover up. Albers magnificent, cool detachment. Mondrian with his separating, and fascinating plus-and-minuses... Pollock (to be serious, was asexual. His involvement was with himself) and his flawless, Mozart-spiritual, Rise-in-the-Flame like the Phoenix orgasmic harmonies based on his mother's exceptional skill as a seamstress.*

In April of 1953, DeKooning had at Janis his first show of the *Women* paintings and in the media cries of praise, my memory says that within the art world, meaning on 10th Street, he was revered because he had paid his dues, and deserved reward, whichever way his work went. *But nobody imitated it! Nobody!* The so-called non-representational stuff, yes...even Bill's paintings in the *Marilyn* series, nobody copied, or used as basis or in *any* way as influence, why? *She was still taboo.*

Around a decade later, on Guston's breaking new ground with recognizable images he was condemned by just about the entire art world, including almost all his friends, for his "return to the figure." *Verboten!* In the creative unconscious the figure is ALWAYS woman. But *he* returned to *another! Worse! SATIRE!!*

In certain circles today, true as ever. The break from the figure created an area of art few understand, but of its own necessity it involves, and in detail, the creative aspects of early years, including high school. And as I type this, March 23, 1990, the editor of *ARTS* Magazine has just rejected a short piece of mine on Franz, and the influence his early, teenage work had on the later, big stuff that made him famous because my proof was "too specialized."

Not only the critics who keep us in the dark, but editors as well. Anyone who does anything new, anything innovative, should beware the first response from the most educated, the most profound minds of the day: dismissal and ridicule.

The meaning of the work of the 10th Street Painters was lost on

---

*More to be written on this, in the future, to be given in appropriate detail. In almost all art no matter what anyone including the artists themselves say, childhood, even early childhood, is crucial in understanding their work.

the media and educated elite, not on the people at large who were pretty sure it was crazy, but in secret saw it was free.

Much, much more to be written on this. The early, preschool work in fingerpainting by kids had a new freshness that still holds and is still exhibited on kitchen doors and walls, as well as in bed and play rooms. The academics shit on it, but in large part, in an expansive, unselfconscious way, people enjoyed its freedom. The masses of imitation Pollocks, and Klines, DeKoonings, broad brushstrokes, drips, bright colors made it fun to do, and in every small-town art show, *in every one,* the "modern" stuff was exhibited as well as still lifes, portraits and traditional landscapes and "primitives." Modern art was here — in the way people thought Picasso was funny. The group of Russian tourists doubled over in laughter looking at the Pollock at the Met, case in point, remember the fun cartoonists had?

The influence of the 10th Street painters was one of freedom and release, because it didn't seem to matter, and it felt good. *Nobody knew what it meant.*

Locked in after WW II, Hiroshima, McCarthy, Korea, beginning of the cold war, and corporate design. No wonder those works, and those artists themselves, are so vivid. They had found freedom in an intuitive development of composition that allowed a new element of chance, and all kinds of sizes with ditto in materials: tar on streets and rain patterns or shadows on sides of buildings anywhere from the Grand Canyon to Chicago, looked a *lot* like that art.

What happened to it and the world after is easy to trace, but if you see where it came from and why, as well as what was done, and what it meant, you'll see how deep we are in a brainwashed, media-educated, enslaved same, same, same world. The painting and drawing and body that emerged from that little 10th Street area, from those few, very different artists, who, in a last thought, it might be seen, in a cross-section pretty well represented this country. Their work was misunderstood, and not at all understood, by anybody even themselves, but remember: the first clue to a happy house and a positive future: kids — nationwide — liked it, *and!* I SAW 'em: watch with keen eyes at what they drew, painted, and sculpted... *because it was what the artists were doing.*

From the beginning it was publicity (in which we took part), word of mouth, or personal letter. Having studied during summer sessions, in high school, at Washington University, I asked the teachers what art school to go to, they said Black Mountain.

For the free spirits across the country, and in the world, who wanted to compose, write or paint or dance or — look, listen and live, on hearing, for over and over that's what it was (John Chamberlain went because Gerry Van de Wiele told him to), no matter if we were stuck at home, away in a college or university and none of it fulfilling, warm in mother-influence without maybe just a shadow of father, or not even that, for a lot of us, and I mean *a lot*, in so much of what he was Olson became that lost, Creative Father, to our infinite reward, making us in that hidden, secret, mountainside blaze of light, like fire: renegades, vanguard creatures that recognized each other in paint, music, language, clay, together in our common effort, in that crystal to be there, to find out what we would discover. That's why we went. There were ads for summer school, in a few papers, and articles by cool names appeared in certain magazines, to give the school another kind of recognition, but that wasn't why we went, we went because we weren't (or were) sure what we wanted, somebody said there's a place in Western North Carolina, and they said the name, in an intuitive move, in the essential curiosity, we went to make the connection, and see just what that would be, take a look at what we had done, or sit around and listen to it, as you do to the experiment, with the long look in your eyes.

That was the *real* reason.

It was not uncommon for people to drift in off the highway, strangers who were not strangers at all, but kindred souls, hungry for that new kind of freedom.

FOOT STEPS

Track backwards—the Russian artist Vladimir Tatlin visited Picasso and Braque in their studios in Paris in 1912.

Tatlin returned to Russia, and could it be that the Constructivist work he became involved with had an influence on the Bauhaus, thus in ways on Albers, and Black Mountain until — Olson, *and a whole new vision?*

Some folks have had great amusement in ridiculing the school for not having a better business sense, the "bread and butter" mentality. Olson and Wes Huss and all concerned tried every way possible, to no avail. Various individuals in the media and at high levels of the Corporate University were vindicated that the school died and pleased they had done their share in watching it go, offering neither hand nor check.

Note what Picasso and Braque did to the form of women: geometric blocks, mechanical cubes, that show at the Modern, walls covered with the feminine shapes transformed into block-objects. Was it revenge against women — *The Woman?*

And loss of father as profound influence, in that bible of Existentialism, *The Stranger,* right at its center Camus has as background in the courtroom scene, *the depiction of another trial: a young man guilty of patricide!* That is no incidental scene! Whether conscious or unconscious, there *it* is: for the language and tone of the final end of the book, of cold nothingness, of no point or reason, is that of a boy in shock from the loss of his father.

"I take SPACE to be the central fact to man born in America, from Folsom cave to now. I spell it large because it comes large here. Large, and without mercy."— Charles Olson, *Call Me Ishmael,* p. 11.

In this troubled world of a lack of identity in kids, and adults (who dress in childish clothes and lounge around in front of their VCRs the way kids used to in sandboxes: the name of the game is entertainment, aw mommy, I *gotta* feel good), not to mention frustration: kids faced with sex and AIDS, adults frustrated and bitter because they've come all this way for so little.

This massive lack of whoness is matched by an inability to express oneself, and to be unable to talk fits real nice into universal televised ignorance. In a consumer society obsessed with it, no one — with the exception of graffiti artists signing their initials across the planet, and ghetto blasters in hand, so we know who's coming down the street — no one seems to care who they are or if they are or if there is anything to say, is there? What is there to say? Who are you? Who am I? Logical questions, with computers for memory, and a calculator in hand to add, subtract, multiply and divide, who by golly *are* you? And me?

We?

One way to confront this would be to establish a system of schools a la Black Mountain, high schools of arts and sciences (some colleges, too), something Olson and I discussed in 1955. Emphasis on the arts: composition, performance and exhibition as basic factor. If art, as Stephen Spender said, is the conquest of self-consciousness, it may well be just the cure for a lack of identity. One school in every neighborhood in the country, any country. Anywhere.

They say that there is nothing new under the sun — Franz said it — somebody somewhere has hit upon it before: all thoughts have been thought, and all the words to be said have been spoken (with, in an effete, very [indignant] much defended: poetic imagination — in its place of course). Who, you can hear the heads of the corporate university growl, would be so vain, to dare claim, anything new, or original, after the grand parade of thinkers, philosophers, and Wise Ones, down the whole high road of human history?

Unh huh.

The one thing that terrifies the educated population is originality. What went on in the 30s, 40s and 50s in a handful of lofts on East 10th Street, and at that school outside Asheville, was, and you may believe still is, a very sore spot, a royal, still very very sensitive Pain in the Ass. Everyone has explained it to everyone's satisfaction, so that no one knows quite what did go on but that's okay, that's — that's the way it was, they were artists, and well, it's pretty crazy.

Thank *God* for Andy Warhol, giving us something we could *see*, and understand! It wasn't Pop and Andy that wiped out the 10th Street work, it was the gleeful media, and you may be sure, in the corporate university... and since the Pop revolution (ignoring the one just before, the real revolution that made art possible for anyone who wanted to do *it and anything creative in any way they wanted*, because at bottom, or once in space all art became in its essence anarchy and, in fine, what was made of it *from what it was* — a bootprint in mud, shards of glass in a gutter... art had become democratic. *Art had become in its highest sense, for anyone who wanted to do it at any age, anywhere* in the world: ANYTHING THEY THOUGHT WAS ART. The first thing to do was *do* it. What happened after would happen after. Throw away the clocks and calendars. Chronos was *gone!* (R.L. Stevenson said the same on taking hikes — a Black Mountain activity, the rule being, as that great writer noted, out walking, do it alone.), since Pop, the razzle-dazzle glitter of technology, reentry of Europe (and a culture we tried to get away from), it's so exciting, or at least distracting, with the media hurtling us into tomorrow with no thought of the past, the idea of great artistic freedom, even as it would predict social changes, for as art follows social change, by its nature it predicts it, and save in illustrative aspects, is never of its so-called present. In artistic thinking — of space, not clocks — the present is transition, and of value only for that, meaning we live in continual spatial transition. Olson's *Mayan Letters*, his sense of the space among the ruins (his punctuation, and poetic narrative, gives a momentum and jolt, forcing re-reading that I enjoyed, like fresh air out of the city, his text is fresh away from even the style, much less dogma, of the educated slaves, in the corporate university) evokes a memory, and in brief, while among those ruins myself, the feeling was of being in a park, in the same style, or arrangement Guston depicted in his paintings in Italy, those strange images, quite like the sense one has in parks *in between* hedges and statues, Guston painted — therefore — *space, as between as well as beside,* which holds true for the Mayan too, meaning a feel of Mediterranean space, very beguiling it is! — so too that of the Mayan. Look at Tulum! It's a park, get it? They put it in space, like all early peoples, *first.* Olson caught that freshness. Guston, too. In the background, way back there, was a desire to in part define through the establishing of its foundation and structure what had gone on and in a natural follow through, tear it apart and rearrange it. Part of that effort is the rearrangement of narrative, by way of a single voice being in truth multiple, but the admission of a divided personality (accepting that as foundation and structure) is in terms of style, undiscovered, but to me, at least, something of a dream which in part this book reveals... it being anything but a smoothrunning story. I'll be sixty in a few weeks, a fact of little meaning save that of this book being a result of a life's involvement since I went to that school, and encountered those persons both there and so soon after, in New York. I was compelled to write the first version, but chose to write this new one, to give me a chance to say, in my amazement, how much I've learned, both there and in memory, as I've continued to write and paint. A student friend, a woman, wrote yesterday (May 22), refusing my use of a page from her journal, which she gave me at school. In it she demands I use my name in the future, in becoming a writer. I had gone into my study one morning, and found it on my desk. *For Fee.*

There is that line about no man is an island, well, as I had the page from her journal, and read it, and no doubt turned, to look out my window over the lake, at the hills beyond, *I had better use that name,* who else was there who would understand how I felt — so proud, moved...

Wasn't *this* why we made our way to New York and to Black Mountain? In the single act of escaping the loving maternal demand in the arts, to create new atemporal images, unrelated to her figure? Images valid only in themselves, even unknown to the artists? Images raised up from the intuitive unconscious that revealed, even *transformed* the artists! Images away from the clock, calendars, the nine-to-five dictatorship of life — *to be free,* and *know not what you paint in a total commitment to its process.*

Franz: "Tell 'em you paint blind."

Anybody who comes up with a new idea is an island, and instant victim of ridicule, in particular in this us (joke) U.S. Jell-o-blab sameness, getting worse, too, for the bland-mob TV sponge-brains developing a widening crust around the edges because in the center the mass media created — entertainment as message and news — mass educated blah, is beginning to lose its personality. A lotta people without personalities. Kinda scary? You bet. Well, that's the future. They'll tell ya no man is an island, sure, like they buy Mozart's Biggest Hits: not because they know — they don't, but because it sounds so good.

Nobody helped me with this. I had no encouragement at home, was unable to talk to anyone, was mocked by a few friends, so I gave up talking. Well, that's good. No, it isn't. Nobody to bounce ideas off of, no good, meaning a *lot* of rewriting, perhaps too much.

To begin and achieve — this book — an event or act that is of originality and challenging ideas — by oneself is unnerving because it demands a logic to justify, or make valid, its premise, which — surprise — *occurs before it is developed, not* the other way around. So the idea, and the development was isolate. I knew through Olson — and agreed with him — that things happen fast in history. The Berlin wall coming down, Gorbachov, Eastern Europe — big changes, very fast, with the arts dormant, asleep. No predictive element there! Well, so be it. Worst of all, nobody to understand, or in truth care, about the completion of this hard work: the complete rewrite of the first version and the deep regression, so creative and edgy, scary, again into the past, toward a point where I knew it would tell me stop. But throughout the trip to Yucatan, and on return, my begging Terry Smith for a new deadline — and getting it — I *had* to bring into full focus everything that was happening, so fast, in an accumulation, one realization after another. I realized on location, first at the ruins south of Tulum (and Tulum itself), the Guston impact, and more, until I *found it* in Olson's *Mayan Letters:* begin in space.

Before established narrative will change, ideas must change, and through a speech involving many varied, still changing ideas, a new formula will present itself for us to follow. We're on the edge of it, have been most of this century, but our problem — and failure — is *we* won't change. And, therefore, we will be stuck with the stylized successful slime that characterizes our bland, and boring, vicious culture.

But a few individuals here and there, including me, *do* change, and I'm not fool enough to overlook, or deny my responsibility in it. *Change must become a discipline.*

Black Mountain, in harmony — at a point and continuing — with the 10th Street action, kept changing as well, until they dispersed, or decentralized, and went out into the world in the figures of their masters and students. Always true, in a great tradition. Having offered an atemporal vision that opened so many doors into space, and FREEDOM! This isolate act is an honor, a labor of love as few know it, for these hearts are mine, and in completion, reward enough.

F.D.
May 23, 1990
New York

Note on this Fishing Group: Key West, 1935–36.
That's my father on the left, and my mother
in the center, seated, in the floppy hat,
holding the name of the ship.

LETTERS FROM MY FATHER TO MY MOTHER: MID-1930s

Thursday evening

Sweetheart:

Its May 10th — and this is our anniversary.

I have an appointment in forty five minutes with a Miss Brooke, one of the field representatives on the Emergency Relief staff. She's a great big girl, like Miss Hackbush, only a much finer personality, and I feel that she's the best friend I have on that staff. I want to talk to her frankly and try and find out just what my standing is over there, — how much chance there is for me to line up with them again, and how to go about it. I feel that she will help me all she can.

But meanwhile I want to talk with you.

Ten years ago right now, — this minute (7:30 PM) we were sitting in that little chop suey place in St. Louis, having our dinner. It was a Saturday evening and I had received my pay from the Shelley Printing Co., ($23.15) and had invested in two tickets to Otis Skinner's "Sancho Panza."

But I'm sure you remember all that just as clearly as I do. How we enjoyed the play, the ride back on the street car to your Aunt Blanch's where you were spending the night. I stopped in for a while before I left you. I'm sure you remember.

We had a whole glorious month together before I left St. Louis to go to New York, — and then that first period of separation while I was trying to save enough money to bring you to me. (Lord, how many times have we gone through that ordeal?)

But you came, and we started off on our own experiment, — there in Gracey's apartment on 26th St. Just look at the two children and you will see how successful the experiment has been.

It has been ten years sweetheart, and while there are certain things I don't like to look back on, — certain things I am ashamed to remember, — the rest has been a wonderful, loving, cherished experience. I am fond of my family and so proud of them. And I am fond of you and particularly proud of my wife. During the past few months as I have made efforts to get lined up in better shape, I have often spoken of "my family in the south," and I always mention you and tell how plucky you have been about it all.

And don't make any mistake. The things I don't like to look back upon are all my own fault. There isn't one thing about you, or these ten years that I can criticize or blame. You have been wonderful.

But there are plenty of things that I criticize and blame myself for. And on this tenth anniversary, sweetheart, I want to apologize for them and to ask you to forgive me. I'm so sorry for so many things. You have taught me so many things. I feel I'm a better man because of you.

And when we get back together, we'll start over, — on the second ten. I hope none of those things will be repeated. I'm going to try and never hurt you again. I hope I can stick to that intention.

And now its time for me to leave. I started off saying that I wanted to talk with you, but I've done more dreaming than talking. And now its time to go. Plug for me during this interview, (I know that you will) — it may develope something.

Goodnight sweetheart. I wish you were here so that I could hold you tightly and kiss you, and tell you that way how fond I am of you.

I was in love with you ten years ago. I think I love you ten times that much now.

Goodnight.

— C —

Friday evening

Sweetheart:

It's just a week today since I have written you a real letter, and I hope this one turns out to be both long and interesting. It's usually hard to tell in advance just how they will turn out in the end.

Well, I'll start off by telling you what I have been doing. I remember of telling you a week ago that I would probably go to the movie that evening. I did. "The Mortal Storm" was good but harrowing. It was the story of the growth of the Nazi movement in Germany with the suffering it brought to one semi-Jewish family. "Alias the Deacon" was terrible.

The next day, Saturday, I phoned Marion and took her out to the Cloisters, but arrived just at five o'clock and found them closed. So we took a ferry across the river at that point, and found a very pretty park on the Jersey side that stretched along the river for a considerable distance. So we had a pleasant walk, came back for dinner at the Greeks, and by that time it was ten o'clock, and I left her. We were both tired.

Sunday I was out with the Talley's, and we finally got down to calling each other by our first names. That is always so difficult for me to start, — I always feel awkward about it. We had a pleasant enough time. Dinner, — and then the Hydes drove me back to the City.

Monday evening I splurged and paid a dollar to see "Tobacco Road". I had never seen it, and it is closing shortly. I know that you don't care for that sort of thing, but I was pretty keen about it.

Tuesday, I spent with Marith, and had a pleasant talk. She expects, but isn't certain, to move to Philadelphia soon, and rent her apartment here. Georgie and Turnley came in before I left, and later, Florie. I wish she had been here while you were here. She is dancing in Al Jolson's new show that opened here in NY last Wednesday, and she had just come from the final rehearsal, — all excited, and yet a bit upset because some fellow had brought her home and had coaxed her to marry him, and had burst out crying when she kidded him about it. Martha Raye (do you know who she is?) is also in the show, and Florie and she have become friends, and she has asked Florie to act as her understudy. Well, that may be an opportunity for her, but I doubt that Florie, as pretty as she is, has really big time stuff in her. But you never can tell.

Wednesday I took Miller and the Hydes over to see Florence. You have probably heard about it. I think they were all interested, but I don't believe any of them were so awfully impressed. Marith was there (asking Florence about her MS.), as I knew she would be. The night before, she had asked me to go with her, and I told her that I would be there with the other people. I didn't feel free to invite her into the party, — it began with a supper at the Hydes apartment, — and she asked me not to speak to her at the hearing, because she didn't want Florence to know that we were acquainted, for some reason. She preferred it that way, and asked me to follow that procedure. However, after her reading, I stopped her as she was leaving and persuaded her to wait for us, and the Hydes drove her home with the rest of us. Miller was to leave the next day, and I suppose she got back there all right.

Last night I spent the evening writing to Mary, and then took the letter over to the main post office in NYC and sent it special. I hope she got it promptly. I hope she is able to get permission from Bobbs Merrill, — and I don't believe it will be difficult to place it with some publisher. If no one else wants it, I'm confident that there are Catholic music houses that would jump at the chance, — and perhaps it would be advisable to submit it to them first.

So that chronological sequence brings me down to today, and here I am spending this evening writing to you, — and how could I do anything better? As I finish, I think I'll take this over to NY as I did Mary's last night, — so you'll get it over the week-end.

I'm enclosing a money order for twenty five dollars. I also sent you twenty five last week-end. You didn't mention it, but I suppose it reached you all right. I like to have you just mention that you receive them, — and then there's no doubt in my mind.

I landed another customer yesterday, — a small metal factory with about 125 employees, — but I was glad to be able to report it to Dr. Prest. We won't do the work for another six weeks, — Oct. 25, — and they have reserved permission to cancel the project if they want to, — but I don't think they will.

I'm enclosing the post card photo that came in the mail yesterday. Do you like it? I didn't like it at all at first, but as I came to study it under the magnifying glass, I began to like it very much. You have a spot under your left eye, that gives it a ghastly effect until you recognize the flaw. I doubt that it is clear enough to be enlarged, — or I would have it done. If you want me to, I will anyway, and we'll see what it looks like. I'm a bit provoked with myself that I didn't have more of these snaps taken during the few days that you were here with me.

Your description of Cara makes me cuss a bit that we aren't together for me to see her development, — and Fee's, and to help you. Of course, I know that they are such wonderful kids, — such good material. And Fee will come along fine too, he's just young now. I'm so glad that Cara has reached the point of helping you, — from now on she should be a big help. She's such a fine girl. And you certainly can be proud of the job you have done with them. — although I don't like the way you speak of "failing in every other effort." Didn't Florence tell you to stop taking the blame for things, and feeling that you were always wrong? Thought you were going to stop that.

I can understand what an emotional ordeal it must have been to have the Kevins go, — but now I wish the new man would come along, and you would be able to settle into a routine. When will he arrive? I'm mighty glad you like him, and I'll bet your work will be easier. With Herm crying over Fee, and me crying over Shirley Temple, and Dr. Kevin crying over his congregation, and this stranger crying because Florie wouldn't marry him, — well, it's an emotional world we males have to face.

Your letter written last Monday said, "I sent you the pictures of Cara today,"— but I haven't received them yet. Are you sure you sent them? Now I wish Ess would take a whole set of pictures of you,— in all sorts of poses,— standing on your head and everything.

You say that Cara is "busy at her school work," so I take it she's over her illness and back at school. I'm glad the teachers think so well of her. I hope she isn't worried any more for fear of not coming up to last years achievements. Talk to her about that, — don't let it worry her. Did the school authorities consent to her taking mechanical drawing?

Everything seems to be going well with me here, and there is no cause for you to worry about me. Dr. Prest told me the other day that "We like you" and then asked me if I would be willing to help on the Health-mobile that is being built. And of course, I assured him that I'd do anything he wanted me to do. My fall activities are opening up now, and I hope I'll be able to bring in some more results. It not only pleases Dr. Prest, — but I think he likes it when he is able to report progress to Mr. Pratt.

I'm comfortable here in my room. I had the army blanket cleaned, and feel more comfortable now, when it crawls up around my neck at night. The last couple of nights it has been cool enough to have half over me and half under. The varnish is gradually being washed out of my new towels, and I'm glad of that. I don't believe I have seen my Olga but once since you left, but we write little notes to each other. The other day I left a note for her asking her to please wash my bath tub out, that it had a ring of dirt around it like a small boy's neck. She answered that she would if I would get some scouring powder, which I did, and now the tub shines. I don't believe she is supposed to do that every day, — but I'm hoping she will.

Fee's photo is pasted up right where you suggested, side of my mirror, and the little fellow is grinning down at me right now. I guess he knows I am writing to you. He grins at me when I comb my hair, or when I tie my neck tie. If I am fussy and particular, he just grins, — or if I am careless and hurried, he just grins just the same. The little rascal is always grinning, — and the funny thing is that I grin back.

And now, — all my love. It's 9:15, and I'll seal this up and take it over to the city to mail. I'll be back here in about an hour, and I expect I'll spend the rest of the evening reading, and so to bed. I have no plans for this week end, tomorrow or Sunday, and I don't know just what I will do with myself. But I'll find something. Our summer hours at the office stop today, and beginning next week I'll be working until 5:15 in the evening, and also on Saturday mornings.

All my love. Keep well. Keep happy. Keep on thinking about me.

— C —

THE BLACK MOUNTAIN BOOK (1970 *Revised*)

TO THE MEMORY OF MY FATHER

"There can be no hearts above the snowline. Oh, ye frozen heavens! look down here. Ye did beget this luckless child, and have abandoned him, ye creative libertines. Here, boy; Ahab's cabin shall be Pip's home henceforth, while Ahab lives. Thou touchest my most inmost centre, boy; thou art tied to me by cords woven of my heart-strings. Come, let's down."

— Melville
Moby Dick

PREFACE

Time is ironic (at Black Mountain there was no time): point of view from the outside world I was there for four years and four and a half summers in a row, and I remember once Charley Olson said he didn't know what irony meant.

He said the iron in it confused him.

When you, or I — we, went between the low white paint-chipped and tilting fences, with the chipped black and white calmly bewitched little sign, that in one of the biggest understatements in my life said BLACK MOUNTAIN COLLEGE, when I passed that, and walked up that gutted dirt road towards the Dininghall, a feminine building (it held a lot), I walked into a different world: a beautiful and violent world of change, and the major thing I learned was

The major thing I learned was how to resent, which I can thank Charley and Franz for, took years to get out of, yes I will explain — later —

But they were great at denouncing books and paintings they hadn't read and seen. Oh, you say I am being resentful? This is unkind because this response is resentful? I should praise them? I'll praise them, to the skies because they were

they were my two fathers.

(1939 Thursday afternoon Dear Fee,

I've just written a birthday note to your sister, — so I'll write a note to you, too. You won't have another birthday until next summer, — but then you'll be ten years old. Well, you certainly are growing up.

When are you going to write me another letter. I like to get your letters, and hope you'll write another one soon.

Do you still have snow on the ground there in Kirkwood, and can you go sliding? I was over at Rockefeller Center this morning, and in between the buildings there is a deep pit, — a whole block long. During the winter, they flood it and let it freeze, and then people go skating there. I stopped to watch them for a couple of minutes this morning as I went by, — some of the people are pretty good skaters, and some were professionals. Many of them wore colored skating costumes, and they looked very nice. But it looked too cold for me, — so I turned up my coat collar, and went inside where they had the heat on. I like to keep my toses, and nosey nice and warm.

Lots of love. I hope everything is going well with you.

Dad)

The most important thing about Black Mountain is (was), the effect it had, because unlike hardly anything else, yet like maybe one thing (the real clue), the whole bunch of us were bewitched. Outside people hated us, and boy they still show their fangs today, and will for years to come, until we and they are dead, and only the myth remains.

We were ahead of them, in our lethal little community in the valley by the lake in the sun.

Now there were outsiders among us: jealousers with university eyes.

The sunny side of life at Black Mountain held its deepest secret sensitivity, intuition, and selfishness. All right, you think I'm being dramatic, all this magic crap. I'm of this world, I'm one of the souls of Black Mountain here, in fact I am Black Mountain. I couldn't cope with this world.

Still can't.

It was several without sides. In fact it had no sides literally. It was wide open in the mountain.

Yes, funny language to describe it. Oh — *invisible,* everything it was — all power flowing up in beauty, it was psychotic: she was out of her head, and we lay in sunshine and smiled.

In a world where Charley Olson sat in a high wooden room, writing as far as I'm concerned the best poems around (except for *The Praises),* bare chested with a blanket draped over his shoulders on a boiling afternoon, while a little man was picking through the stones and tall grass at the edge of the lake finding the oldest fossils in history, while Nick Cernovich, Franz and I, in a rowboat, were trying as quietly as possible to get as close as we could to that white egret which stood in the shallows near the island — the cattle roamed the mountainside, *that* was WONDERFUL — *our wonderful world.*

The nights closed *in,* dark as jungle nights as I, barefoot, gingerly made my way down the dark stony dirt road (I just got a whiff of that), fearing something *archaic* as the world I walked in.

I also feared the rattlesnakes (me too) stretched out on the road warming their bellies, and the whizzing bats, just missing my face.

Those deep black southern moonless nights, and then — blaze of dawn creeping down the mountains, and as I sat by the lake, reborn every morning barefoot barechested beautiful in bluejeans (no underpants, none of us wore underpants) (some of the girls didn't either), I rolled a cigarette, sleepily sipped homebrew thinking fuck French class *I* was aware of my identity gathering in the universe.

Before I left to go into the army, my senses rose so fully I felt of religion, and abstraction — clear through me — oh I did fear commitment to us — like later, the nights on the world troopship sailing to Bremerhaven, I sitting emotionally on the metal steps reading by the red fire bulb the first line of Charley's great poem *The Kingfishers*

"What does not change / is the will to change"

We were all crazy.
I was afraid of everybody.
The lake was polluted.
I couldn't ever leave. I had to sit on those boulders on top of the mountain and gaze down through the clouds — remember when

we put barbed wire around the property? Couple hundred acres up and down the mountain so the cows couldn't get away.

They did anyway.

Chickens are the dumbest creatures. Cows next.

Listen to me! — we'd start off at dawn, some of us hungover and with a pack horse, tools and the roll of barbed wire, *we made our way up the mountain.* Through the trees: I could find my way now. There was a sagging barbed wire fence we had to duck under. The students with the horse went another way, I think, but beyond that the world changed into a jungle of rhododendron. We went up a steep rise, and there was — what's the word —

reservoir

grey mouldy solid concrete, the water
oh the water was delicious.

dark, ice cold: and sipping it I smelled a smell I will never smell again, *it sank in me,* my senses got so sharp I felt the air touch the back of my skull: cool, still moist pressure.

I rose and went zig zag through a rising green corridor of trees with the sun pouring through. It was very steep, very hard to get up, and the Goddamned roll of barbed wire, the horse was with us, I think it was an old horse, poor, tired and it took one look at those slippery rocks and said well fuck that.

"Give the horse a rest," Doyle said, he was the farmer at school, "he's tired."

"He's always tired," somebody muttered. We laughed.

But once up it, the great reward was ahead as we went through a narrow place single file, took a sharp left through a doorway into the start of a rising sunny blue world.

Of long swaying grass to the top of the mountain, and the great dark boulders.

We waded through the grass, got to the top and went to work.

At lunch we sat in a shaded area and made a fire, and made coffee: passed sandwiches around *boy* they were good, rolled up

some Bull Durham, and gazed down through the clouds at her —
and clear across the floor of her beautiful valley to the Seven Sisters
Mountains sipping boiling hot coffee — blended with a little fresh
farm cream...

On summer mornings in Pennsylvania when I was six, I went to
the orchard in the valley for apples for the pigs (Jesse gave me a
little bucket). I picked apples off the ground and smelled them,
carefully inspecting them because they were so pitted and partly
rotten. Then I picked from the trees, and when my bucket was full
I lay in the grass, arms out, and watched tops of grass blades bend
in the breeze before my eyes. The sun twinkled and blurred as
blade tips touched and drifted apart. I watched the bees race through
the breezes. I have always loved bees, I love bees. Little spiders
floated by, windblown on delicate webs. I perceived the distance
from my eyes to the tips of the grass blades, and from there to the
sailing spiders — and gnats and flies, deeply moved by the distance all the way up to the clouds, in the sky where the sun was.

When I was four years old, I stood at water's edge on the beach at
Key West, Florida, and gazed out at the Atlantic. I thought the sky
and surface of the Ocean met, far out, because the straight dark
line of the breakwater indicated it. I liked that.

It's simple. I was at Black Mountain before I got there.

THE WART

Towards the end of my first year a wart appeared on the top of my right wrist, and I began a habitual picking at it. Sometimes until it bled.

One of the two cooks, Corny, by nickname, boy could SHE write a book! She was there when I begged that art teacher to hit me, and when he did, and I wept, I remember the pain in her eyes. He stormed out of the kitchen in disgust, and she came to me as I got up, took my arm and led me back by the stoves, gave me a paper cup of Malrey's homemade peach brandy, and said (I hear her tender voice) I must take care of myself.

"You're driving yourself crazy."

It was true. (I couldn't drive anybody else crazy.)

One sunny afternoon she beckoned me to join her by the sink, and with a wink showed me a piece of thread, about six inches long. She said she was going to get rid of that wart.

We went out behind the Dininghall, a few steps around near the apple tree by the lake, and she began to tie the thread around the wart, but because we were laughing so hard, it wouldn't tie right. She said it didn't want to go on. But finally she was able to get it around with a knot, a chancey knot, and then, I can't remember clearly what — she waved her hand over my wart, she sprinkled some dirt on it, and we closed our eyes and chanted Go away wart. Go away wart. Go away wart. We opened our eyes, it was still there, and she jumped to a patch of grass. I also, and as she instructed, dug a very small hole. She took off the little circle of thread as if it was hot, and quickly dropped it in the hole. We covered the hole, and stood up. She looked at me, eyes bright.

"It's a tough one, so we'll give it awhile: say two weeks."

I put a few pebbles around the spot.

Two weeks later we went out, laughing: me picking at my wart, she saying something went wrong.

The thread was gone.

We doubled over with laughter, and she whispered,

"Oh that's a *bad* wart."

Franz had been invited down to teach painting in August of 1952. The disappearing thread incident was in the spring of 1950. So two and a half years later, after saying a very emotional so long to Franz and Nancy at the station, one September morning I was brushing my teeth, shaving, etc., and I looked down at the wart. In a flash of hate of it, and anger at myself and a deep — deep and ugly disgust of *it on me,* I wanted it off. Tentative, I picked at it. A piece came off; then another piece.

With my thumb I rubbed it off. My wrist was clean and that's the end of it.

THE HORNED BEETLE

Charley's writing classes were on Monday nights in the Studies Building.
 The room was rectangular and windows lined the left wall. The blackboard was a creamy white and the tray held blue chalk; in the daytime, in that room, you could see outside clear up the side of the mountain to the Pasture where cows and chickens walked around. I had a French class in that room, one year, and the animals distracted me. I mean, I wanted to be — do that, be a chicken which I am anyway, I am, free as a chicken, and fuck French — au revoir period — although a chicken's freedom —
 When Tommy wasn't playing the last movement of Beethoven's Ninth so loud we had to pound on the wall to tell him to turn it down, maybe he came to Charley's class once in a while, and sometimes with a gallon of moonshine. The room filled with smoke and we drank from the jug and Charley said things like, and this is what quotation marks are for, to open it, which is as far as I'm allowed to get,
 "You're your own train, you got your own track, and you can go anywhere."
 Mary used to bring Airwick and the way she put it on the long table made her place formal. God I loved her, and it was a dream. The windows — it wasn't her
 it was made out of me
 The windows were big and one opened so that whatever breeze there was came in, if we left the door open. But sometimes there wasn't a breeze. And sometimes there was — anyway wonderful when Mary angrily cried out,

"It's too Goddamned smoky in here!"

And we sat in still smoke and drank moonshine and listened to Charley talking about World History and himself, and us, and it happened a few times, about me, which embarrassed and frightened me. Short pants. But then he got on that damned thing about me knowing all about Faulkner. I had read a lot of Faulkner when I was twenty and twenty-one.

He never liked Faulkner, if you will, and so any time anybody ever mentioned Faulkner, in a gesture he'd tie it to me. Four years is a long time, in or out, and except when he was in Yucatan, Charley, God it got to be a fuckin' drag, and around the fourth year, after I had lost my wart, I made a complaint.

"Listen, Olson,"

we called him by his last name, and that's something I can't figure out: in fact it's hung me up for years. And then, when somebody showed up from outside, and shook hands with Charley and called him Charles, I was shocked. Hey — that's not Charles, that's OLSON. Six feet seven, and I struck him out with the bases loaded in the clutch. Boy was he mad. He threw his bat in the bushes, cursed me, and stormed off the field. I can see me now. Doubled up in laughter on the pitcher's mound, terrified.

His chest was so big he couldn't get his arms around, and with two outs in the bottom of the last inning, my heart in my mouth on a three and two count, the tying run Ben Shahn on second
third

I made my windmill delivery rifling a high inside fastball, and he just couldn't hit it, and he knew it before he swung. But he had to swing, even when he knew he was out, so he did and he missed: we won. He lost — his team lost and if I can stop chuckling

Does Charley think it's funny?

He's mad right now, there in London remembering that son of a bitch from Missouri struck me out.

I stuttered, vowels were painful at the beginning of a sentence.

"I-I've read other things than FAULKNER!"

Who was it used to call him Charles? Later I asked him, in Buffalo, if he liked being called Charley. He was enthusiastic (me too). Was it Duck?
YES! Get on!
Charley said Man is vertical, and when I told him that the minister in Kirkwood, Charles Kean, told me that the Cross was minus made plus I disagreed and said the opposite, because I had the image of a vertical man striding forward through lateral, or horizontal, forces, like religion, and time. Charley liked what I had to say to the minister which at that time pleased me, but later I was troubled, and for a long while. Why did Charley avoid his feelings for religion in his Maximus Letters? I still see him, or us, on the dirt roads, or the scrub ball diamond, walking, but I see it now as us moving through an energy-field, with a voice of a sense of religion—which I'll never deny again—results of and response to—experience, and the two sticks of the Cross become a reminder of one deep happenstance that can maybe relate to the inside future, in the form of winds, or more accurately, breezes, so as we move forward we create a stir in a place that was still — invisible, but so raw, so energetic it appeared to be a void, even to Jung, yet to us it was active, and we called it space, and got it going. Strong Black Mountain.
Charley's classes were great, and they as if never stopped. He was the best teacher, he gave it everything he had. He gave it himself, he gave Black Mountain him — in fact he was Black Mountain. But when he couldn't interpret a dream he had had around 1950, and when the school began to go broke in late 1955, he made a move which foretold the end. He withdrew into his house working completely on the Maximus Letters. I visited after I got out of the Army, it was so sad and lost without him walking around. There was no order, and everything I had loved, all my secret places, deserted jungle. It wasn't mine any more. I had it in my heart, though, and in my memory, and sometimes I feel that when I die a last breeze will slip from between my lips and float up and disappear into the grand air of the universe, timelessly alive amid

the stars, the sun, and the moon, in a whisper, *Black Mountain*, forever: as Kalahari Bushmen knew.

Classes began around seven thirty and sometimes went on until midnight, and sometimes, after they were over, we'd all walk down to the Dininghall, open the screendoor in back and go through the small corridor into the kitchen and sit around eating peanut butter sandwiches and drinking milk or coffee and listen to Charley talk about the Roosevelt days. John Dierkes told me Roosevelt loved Charley.... Dierkes' face shone: opened his hands when he said the word loved: and in the kitchen as Charley talked about FDR Charley's face softened, his eyes were warm, brilliant...

Every now and again on days when I sat on the bench under the tree in front of the Dininghall, my bare feet up on the millstone, I'd see a black Chevvy come rocking up the road, pass me, and pull to a stop outside the Office.

I knew.

Two men got out, two men in black suits, black shoes, black snap brim hats, black ties, and white shirts. White world men.

Bad news.

They had come to see Charley.

They went to his house, and a while later came out, and, getting into their car, quietly and without a trace of dignity, they left. I was visible to them, quite clearly, but they didn't want to look, probably the case, that half naked young figure sitting under that tree with his feet rather airily crossed on that round piece of history. Even without their having read anything, it was obvious who they thought I was, felt who I was in spite of them, quite so, and because feelings is a word they never use, their exit might read,

"Let's get out of here. See that kid?"

"Okay! I'll start the car."

I watched their two similar heads in the front seat roll by. My eyes in slits. Smoke curled from my nose.

After a while Charley would appear, and we'd go into the Dininghall, get a cup of coffee together and go sit on the porch, gaze over the lake and not talk. When I grinned and said his two friends had come for a visit again, he sometimes snickered and he sometimes scowled: depending on what they asked, depending on what he told them. He never told me what went on, never at length, anyway.

Once I pressed him. His fast answering look came so straight into my eyes, and hit so deep, my eyes changed, while he slowly and subtly shook his head. Franz was like that, too, but Franz would speak, and softly:

"No, Fee."

Sometimes my eyes would tear. God, I missed my father.

We sat around the long table, and Charley sat at the head, in front of the white blackboard. I often sat, as it happened, at the opposite end.

Paul Goodman had given Tim a dog, she was a great dog, red, Tinkerbelle, and there was one thing that infuriated her. She didn't care about being knocked down, stepped on or screamed at, but when you rubbed her hair the wrong way she went berserk, boy could she bark! Now and then, in Charley's class when things were going along, somebody who was patting Tinkerbelle, would do that wrong thing. She'd come off the floor — straight up — with an earsplitting bark into a whirling blur of rage, standing on one foot in the air, teeth bared after the hand — then she'd fall into her heap on the floor and it was over, while we put our ears and eyes back on. Tinkerbelle was buried right next to where the thread had vanished. By the apple tree.

Charley was an enthusiastic teacher, and in those days optimistic, completely absorbed in his talk: the white blackboard began to fill with blue diagrams, blue words and long blue sentences, his hands turned blue and he had blue smudges on his face and mustache from smoking his cigar with his chalk hand, on he went, and once, with no place to write, he wrote towards the edge of the blackboard, wrote down the right margin, there was no right margin, but he went on, crossing over and going through already written sentences until he came to the chalk tray, and bending over, went clean off the blackboard to the floor, laughing with us.

Outside it was dark, and except for the light cast from the neon tubing on the ceiling which caught branches and leaves, beyond that the mountain rose in the night, and in the summer the white light drew moths that swirled around the neon tubes, also June bugs which fell upside down wiggling on our books and papers: also flies, mosquitoes, and strange narrow transparent insects came in too, and darted near our faces in the smoke. But one insect terrified me — the horned beetle coming in through the window like a slow moving bullet, wings clattering: bounced off walls with sharp ugly sounds, recovered, took off again and came at us. It was big, two, three inches long, almost an inch wide: serrated legs and claws, its black horned head protruded off its broad humped glossy shoulders, large wings like metal blades. Impossible to concentrate on what Charley was saying, because I felt that beetle had a message for me, it always seemed to choose me, and as Charley talked and asked questions and argued I was ducking and swinging, I knocked the beetle away in the air, it tumbled onto the table, someone knocked it on the floor, you'd have to have boots to step on it, sneakers were impossible, and as most of us wore sandals or sneakers or went barefoot, myself, anyway, my skin crawled, and I began a slow fear of Charley's summer classes. Nobody else liked that horned beetle either, we were all apprehensive when it came in — it was really ugly, brute ugly, archaic, ugh. Awful. Once I kicked it into the hall and closed the door, and once, I missed a swing at it and it landed, claws out, on my forehead. I rose from my chair, slapping my head, smashed its shell but it stuck there! I took it in my hand and squeezed, tore it off and felt it crackle and writhe against my palm. I flung it onto the floor — sat down crimson-faced, rubbing my forehead, hard, covering my eyes to hide my tears.

THE BEE

Two two-storey wooden buildings, North and South Lodges, were where the students lived: girls in North Lodge, boys in South Lodge. Beyond the front porch of South Lodge a grassy area gradually descended to tall grass and woods: in the woods was the contemporary, one room, window-walled little house called Music House, where I used to practice my trumpet. Beyond, the fence ran along the road.

The washing machine was underneath South Lodge, and the wives and girls and boys would lay the wet laundry out on the grass and read, sun ourselves and talk until it dried.

Once Harvey and I were waiting for his laundry to dry, sitting cross legged, drinking coffee and talking. It was a bright warm day, with a little breeze.

A bee zipped in front of my face, and hung there, buzzing, about six inches away from my eyes: a black and yellow striped bumblebee, fuzzy and fat — full of curiosity. I focused on it, smiling.

"It thinks you're a flower," Harvey murmured.

The bee flashed off — about twenty feet away to my left, and hung there. A moving blurred spot. Then it came back, zip, and hung, suspended, buzzing, adjusting to the breeze, in front of my eyes. It flashed away again, and after a moment, as if on a string, shot back. But I had moved my head a little, to test it: it came to where I had moved. I moved my head to the left, it followed, to the right the same, and hung, tremulous, glittering in the sun.

"What do you want?" I asked, and the bee was silent.

"I do love you," I said. The bee was silent.

In a wink it slanted away on a breeze, and I watched it rise until it was out of sight in the treetops.

THE BEE AND DAN

I encountered Dan on the concrete deck in front of the Studies Building. He seemed a little faint. I asked him if anything was wrong and he said he didn't know, but that he had just been stung by a bee.

His normally clear crystal blue eyes with black target centers blurred; he put a hand on the white fence post. I looked at him, startled. His feet were half red, from the toes back. In a matter of a minute his feet were all red. I can't remember — but Charley's wife Connie was getting Dan into the car. He was almost unconscious. His ankles were red. Connie's face at the wheel was drawn with anxiety as the car disappeared around the turn.

She raced into the town of Black Mountain, the doctor lay him on the table, and fast as he could injected him with adrenalin and calcium and saved Dan's life — red to his ribs.

FROM ACROSS THE VALLEY

I was walking down the road towards the Dininghall one afternoon when I felt a hard, narrow breeze cross my forehead, very close, in a high pitched diminishing whine. I kept walking, puzzled by the sound, feeling a strong skin contraction and chill in my temples. WOW! *My brain was trembling!* I sat under a tree in shock, and thought about *that!*

THE RATTLESNAKE IN THE DOORWAY, KITTY, HITLER, AND THE LIBERAL-KILLERS

I walked towards the door to the Studies Building and saw a rattlesnake, straight out, on the threshold: just inside the building the white haired Communist lady watched with an angry expression, muttering somebody should get that thing out of here, and from behind me, I felt his warm hand on my bare back, I heard The Man Who Had Escaped Hitler chuckle, and say, rather sarcastically, in German,

"So. A rattlesnake in the doorway."

The musclebound boy from the farm came on the run with a long stick, and threw the rattlesnake over the parapet into the bushes by the Library: we sat on the concrete deck in the sun and laughed and talked about snakes.

Once a week I walked down the long dark corridor of the bottom floor of the Studies Building at night and knocked on his door: he let me in and we drank and fucked and he told me stories about Hitler, and how he had escaped Germany and returned with the Americans and gotten revenge. His dog bit me and he laughed, the sadistic bastard — showing alarm only when I wept, boy I fucked him good one night. I wrote a story about him *(Warm Simplicity)*. Don't tell it.

Another night the boy from the farm came in my room, he slid into bed next to me; he smelled of grass and hay. We embraced. It didn't work out. He thought he was gay and he was, but NEVER tender: about a year later he left school and a year later came back, said he'd met a boy in Annapolis who worked miracles in sixty-nine.

One day he put a dead rat in the flower pot in the reading room to scare the Librarian. It scared me, too.

The Librarian was an older woman, stockily built, and very kind. I think I liked her too much: yet afraid of her dreamy figure, and she had that forward tilt that age brings. She walked a little like Disraeli, or with a hint of Lincoln in very old age, climbing steps slowly — though she could move fast when she wanted to. Not long after school folded, she died, and though I didn't show it, I was very hurt, and regretted not having known her better. Her hair was white and wispy. She wore it piled up on her head, like my mother used to, and when she tucked loose hair back in place, which she did all the time, those raised arms and raised breasts struck me so deeply I had to turn away. Eyes lowered. She used to serve afternoon tea in her apartment: a sunny clean wood room. Her name was Nell.

Most of those years there weren't any girls. I hated those guys kissing me, but the times with *him* — look, come and go, but don't stay too long — the times with him were, even then, interesting and rewarding. It was the only rewarding relationship I've ever had with a man (you've got a bad memory). Well, yes, there was the boy in highschool, and that was all right. He made those beautiful model airplanes, and I thought to myself, What can I do to get one? There was one special plane, the FW190. I think I still have it. At home. But the capers by the Meramec River when I was in the Seventh Grade weren't so great: why do I keep thinking they were? His prick was so dirty! I liked lying on the river wharf, though, flies open, watching the motor boats and marking twain in the sunny day away skipping school, Red Head and I, also watching across the river, other kids swimming at the foot of houses on stilts in the water and I remember a dream!

I went down an embankment and saw people playing in a river

at the foot of houses on stilts in the water. But the roofs were thatch, oh *they* were savage folk. That orgy at Black Mountain — I left fast, I hated it. Those guys crawling all over each other, naked and sucking and kissing, and me, angry and frightened in that little house with the lights out at the foot of the mountain, that night.

Remember the night that hungry boy came into my room and we got drunk and he was wet, and trembling?

We fell cross ways on my bed and began. He said afterwards it was the first time. I laughed: Where have you been? Why, you mean, you didn't know you were queer? Wow. Strangely enough, the sex was good. Boy did he need it. Previously we hadn't been very close, and even afterwards weren't. But we had a secret, and I won't tell anybody his name.

Oh yes and then years and years later he called up and said Hitler was in town, did I want to see him? So Hitler had been talking, and I stuttered and then angrily said,

"Hell no," worldly, "I'm married!"

Very well, I say bitterly to hurt yourself and pretend that game, remember the night in the shadows under the tree by the place where you saw the bee? Kitty was furious at you: *"Cut this faggot game out, Fee Dawson, you're not queer. Stop hurting him!"*

Kitty, tall with grey wavy hair and a pock-marked face. Slender and lithe, and LOVED to dance, boy that guy was one hundred percent faggot, and he was *very* funny, also sad. I learned a world from him, I even knew that ever changing language. Kitty, dear, how are you? I remember. I see your face before me, and as I remember the maypole afternoon with the girls, I see you with a garland of flowers in your hair, the vines over your dancing body, dancing around and around the maypole, weaving in and out among us, as we sang and drank wine, all of us Olson too, with flowers in our hair, the girls were so beautiful, the sun was bright, the sky was blue. Oh we danced! We danced and danced! And we sang and drank wine! Really, it was splendid, you and Farmboy, and Hitler, the Serbian Dancer, and me, and the girls — that New York Blonde Piano Player!

Kitty had class, he had real style: learned it from those USC football players that hung around Hollywood, and the costume Kitty made for the party, the theme being what the well dressed gentleman will wear in the Year 2500, was a knockout. We used to work hard on the parties, beginning to drink around noon. Drawing class from one to four made me anxious. How could I think about art when I had to work on my costume? My God, remember that party where the girl jumped naked out of the cake? Kitty worked for weeks on that cake — plaster over cardboard, wouldn't show it to anybody. He was a potter. I can hear his voice, say at supper, as he gazed languidly across the table at the Serbian Dancer, asking him in a throaty voice, accent the you, "What do you do?" and the Serb responding, in kind, softly, underlining the I, "I, dance; what do *you* do?" Kitty always spaced his words, answered with a two-word song, above his outflung arms, "I, POT!"

His high pitched laugh "Okay you guys," slid down into butch, "eat." We obeyed.

Most of us had gathered at the far end of the Dininghall, in our costumes, and were drinking and talking, and dancing, under blue and green overhead spotlights, listening to the same old songs on the record player.

At the opposite end, near the kitchen, there was a partition, behind which the coffee urn and storage cabinets, and in a curving run Kitty swept around the partition into full view,

"YOO HOO! GIRLS!"

Did a pirouette, stopped: posed for all to see.

Dressed from head to ankles in skin-tight light blue green leotards: gold painted sneakers on his feet: a blue green cap that covered his head completely but for his face and ears, he had big ears, and as he made his way forward in slow leaps, he moved his arms waving his golden wings.

Of shining slender copper tubing with an open gold thread crisscross structure. The wings rose above his head, about three feet long, yet curved outward from his shoulder blades, twinkling in the spotlights, and from the tip of each wing, at the end of a thread, hung one half of a ping-pong ball. In his outstretched right hand he held, by one finger, a half gallon jug of the red wine he loved, he leaped, and when he landed, threw out his arms, tossed his head and again called out a soprano, adding, *"OHHhhh..."*

"I'm HERE!" Rushing toward us, into our arms — with laughter and affection, we embraced and kissed him, admiring his wonderful costume.

But as at all the parties, we of course continued dancing, and drinking, gathering speed: we danced deep into the night, and then went home, or slumped on the Dininghall floor, or madly banged on the piano, or fell asleep by the lake — we Steppenwolves moved towards dawn in modern loneliness, anger and frustration, it was all so sad and pointless, as the release of my fury found in my constant masturbation after parties, lying in my filthy bed alone.

On a handful of Sunday mornings — we knew it was Sunday because there had been a party the night before, and because the air was different. I always knew: kind of special Sunday pointlessness. Also because the food was that Sunday crap, and damned little of it. Sunday was, except for the buildings, the only thing left over from the Old Years, and because Charley and all of us had changed that, the residue really burned me up. Lunch, was it supper? was, like a picnic, that the Liberals from the Forties gave us. They got it from the Thirties, where it started in Europe. It's called a custom — oh yes, there were MORE! I forgot! We had to dress for Saturday night supper! Christ Almighty SUNDAY SCHOOL, boy when Black Mountain was bad it was terrible, proof being I got to like dressing up, being civilized a couple of hours every week: in fact it was kind of fun, switching back out. Also in the institution-hangover: every study — in the Studies Building — had a number, a white number, painted by the door in the hallway. Bert tried to wash it off but it wouldn't come off. Somebody raised a fuss. It didn't bother me much, for some reason. And there were a couple of funny Liberals there, there are always a couple at places like that, saying Bert's number was just a designation, etc.

Every now and again a Liberal showed up to teach. That poor social anthropologist and his pretty wife left fast, went down the road in shock. They had sat before the student body, some of the faculty stood around, as the social anthropologist tried to answer our questions: because the guy had never heard of Frobenius we wiped him out. His weak theories, limited possession of source material, lack of fieldwork and almost total lack of feeling for literature and the plastic arts, was the end of him. We sat silently, coldly staring at him. Lunch followed, and I see the sad fella yet, sitting at lunch, almost in tears, beside his stunned wife, while half naked killers ate salad, lentil soup and homemade bread. After lunch one of the faculty smiled in pity and a muted really very sorry, shook the guy's hand, and they left: stumbled towards their car, got in, and drove away. We sat on the porch, feet up on the rail and watched them go.

One guy — one Liberal — made it in. Hitler had gotten fed up with being broke, so he got a job somewhere else. Sent me Christmas cards with a Hallmark type poem, but inside he pasted a glossy photo of his dog, message on the facing page: Would you care to step into my office? Old Adolf.

The Liberal guy who made it as Hitler's replacement was very clever, yes, and fat, well, he paid for his cleverness. We found out what *he* was, one of those cats who admired that Princeton anthropologist who never did any fieldwork, and very quickly he began to think twice about his fortune. Nobody went to his classes, and except for a couple of other Liberals, he ate alone, and except for the times we played with him (shot him down for fun), he hardly spoke to us.

When he left it was in a dark cloud down the road in a taxicab with a pipe in its mouth: we napped on the grass.

She came out of North Lodge, walked down the steps. In bluejeans, tee shirt, sneakers no socks: had just washed her hair, beautiful blonde, silken, her skin soft and white and pink: she was lovely, and as I approached her smiling, her eyes glittered. I stopped in my tracks, "Hi," caught in my throat reading her mood message *dot dot dit keep away from me dot dot dash I kill.* She passed by me and sat on the grass in front of the Dininghall and shook her hair loose to dry.

On a couple of Sunday mornings we sat at the piano in the (deserted) Dininghall; she played while I played trumpet; she sang and I kept saying things like wait, wait, and we'd go back: it was hard to play because I was laughing so. Onward Christian Soldiers was tough for beginners — she did the transposing.

She tossed her head and sang, and sitting beside her on those incredible mornings playing music, was music: the sun streaming in on two college kids from the middle class remembering Sunday School — as I write — we're *there!*

THE UPPER LEFT HAND CORNER

The woman who walked on a slant was charming and very clever: I liked her: we had a good thing going. She was the Head of Admissions. I was one of two students on Admissions, and with the aid of the Business Manager we decided which student applicants would come to school. One spring day I gazed at the small glossy photo of a fine looking blonde girl scientist who wanted to come to the College. We read her application thoroughly, etc., and I hungrily voted yes. Head of Admissions smiled. And several months later I walked out of South Lodge and headed towards North Lodge, passing the Office, and as I veered right towards the Dininghall, it was a warm yet cool crispy September day, and I saw a station wagon parked in front of North Lodge, tailgate down, and there was a blonde girl in a white dress taking suitcases out of the back. I rushed to her aid with a laugh, and introduced myself, and when we shook hands and she said her name I winked and told her I already knew. *Soon after we fucked,* but it was not to last. One of Joe's students, on a visit to Mexico before coming to Black Mountain, had contracted malaria, which recurred. She cared for him, day by day, for several months, until he was well. It was the fall of 1952, after the Kline/Tworkov summer: I'll never forget her. Hope she's still on her motorcycle (as she wrote me), going up and down hills and valleys. I drew her: she used to pose for me. But by then I had fallen for a beautiful Jewish girl, just sixteen who had come into my arms at a dance, which we left, and ended up in my study...

They both posed for me.

When Philip Guston saw my drawings, he expressed enthusiasm —

"Come to New York and see *my* work!"

Which in fact I did.

I had a study where I wrote and slept, and drank tea or coffee and listened to Woody Herman, Stan Kenton, Lenny Tristano, Miles, Getz, with Neil and Ken Noland, and Dan Rice, drinking home brew that Basil and Bert made, and got sick, the shits all next day.

In my study where I hummed and whistled Tea for Two, fascinated by the change of key in the bridge, I looked out the window at the lake wishing I could write the book I wanted with BIG letters and a glass clean narrative, listening to the ducks. My Blonde Piano Player who still loved me was drinking tea and gazing at my drawings on the wall.

One afternoon I filled an empty gin bottle full of water, filled two glasses and we sipped, and as we got drunk, we sat close, the sun poured in the window and out through my open doorway I saw across the hall into my painting study, and out that window I saw the light on the mountain, as I sat beside my Blonde, dust motes slowly tumbled and sifted through rays of sunlight, she merged with me and I with her, she in my bluejeans and I in her bluejeans and tee shirt, sipping gin and leaning against each other until the distant sound from across the lake — the supper gong, and we rose and walked down the corridor slowly separating, and when we were on the road, we were apart, heads splitting.

To return together in the nights, in the boat on the lake. We drank homebrew out of mason jars and got drunk and sang and each kissed, across the gulf of darkness in a slow upward rising of spirits entwined, I rowed she rowed we rowed. I kissed her as she, and she as me murmuring frog songs, crickets and the night birds: ultra conscious bats in whispering trees around each other whispering: blades of grass like us. The mountain rose in a basso crash. Late. Late. We kissed. We rowed. We rowed in, and parted on the steps of North Lodge. I went to my room. I slept and dreamed I

saw a lake in a valley. A boat was on the lake. Two were in it, side by side of one. Yellow hair, soft breasted/soft hair on upper lip and chin.
   I grew a beard.
   "You look like Jesus!" cried the girl in the dime store at home. Christmas vacation 1952. She later ran away to Cuba with a lover. JoAnne Cunningham.
   I found my center in drawing class, and although it can change, it appeared that, as I drew with my right hand, I was aware of my left, like Guston.

   (1939   Dear Dad
   Aunty Dot bought me a teddy bear and I named it butterscotch! it is so cute you just ought to see it. by the way how are you getting along? I hope you are getting along better. Well by golly I'm just getting along swell in scholl. The other day in scholl we made finger paintings mine was "tornado over the Picific" Miss Trilift our art teacher made a finger painting of a "jungle scene" it was really good. Mom tells me you are getting along swell. And by the way thanks a lot for the note I appreciate it very much. singing off
                                    Fee)

   The classes were held in a sagging one story building left over from the Second War: then, students could look up and see what was going on in the Studies Building so they called it the Eye. We sat in chairs with drawing boards, newsprint tacked on, braced up on other chairs. Classes were three hours long. Joe Fiore was the teacher: they were *the best*.
   The first class Joe told us, "Look at the paper. Don't draw yet. I'll tell you when you can begin."
   He then said we could make one vertical line. One vertical line, nothing else. No curves, circles, etc., and not until he gave the word.
   I shifted uneasily in my seat and looked at the paper, and looked out the window. I looked at the 18 x 24" paper thumbtacked on the horizontally turned drawing board tilted on a chair before me. I gazed at it off and on for around an hour, and got lost in it. I began to see possibilities, the paper came clear. I focused on the

visual counterpart of mathematical center, feeling it shift up and down yet move right and left. I looked to the bottom of center, no, and the top, no, and getting warm I looked to the upper right hand corner, no, the lower right corner, no, the lower left, not quite — but close. I looked to the upper left hand corner and hit. With my left hand in the air, my right hand lightly holding the pencil just off the surface, I tested that area and then tested the previous areas, and tested them again, and kept returning to the upper left hand corner, about six to eight inches down and in, and in a gathering conclusion, I knew I would begin where the paper stood out. My right hand poised over that place.

"Okay," Joe said. "Make the mark."

I made a decisive three to four inch vertical line, sat back, and looked at it.

After three hours of the next class we made two vertical lines: next class three: the fourth class we were allowed to make three vertical lines and one horizontal line. Always after three hours. I got to know that paper field, and though ever since have gradually moved around mathematical center, the most rewarding line yet moves as if from the upper left hand corner, and I at last understood Mondrian: the early work, in a final separation from her, as she would want — in admiration. Anyway, it was the end, which she knew, no matter how we felt. "You are the artist, you are the poet, you are the lover," she wrote me, after I got out of the Army, none without the other... Does she still have her motorcycle? I don't know. I hope so. I heard she went on with her science. Where is she? I don't know.

POISON IVY

A couple of years after the old Chem Lab burned down, Paul Williams and Dan Rice designed a new one: a box-like structure nestled among trees, projecting off the mountain, overlooking the road and the lake, between the Dininghall and the Studies Building. One of the first things we did was to clear shrubs, etc. I, barefeet in shabby boots, tore out vines, shrubs, moved logs, etc. That night I sat on my bed feeling funny, tired, in a daze. I looked down at my right boot.

It was lopsided: laces pulled taut, way out of shape. Gently I untied the laces, and in pain and itch I got the boot off.

I gaped, horrified.

My foot was covered with blisters.

One on top, as big as an egg. I took off the other boot. Same thing. Both feet covered with giant blisters, huge ones, my feet were grotesque: toes puffed and almost glued together by blister clusters: the top of each foot a nightmare. I wanted to cry! A knock on my door, which opened, and the Serbian Dancer came in, saw my foot! Gasped, and put his arms around me: in fact it was he who took care of me. The doctor prescribed footbaths, and I went back to the old calamine lotion, no help, but my nurse brought me breakfast, lunch and supper as I lay in bed, the first couple of days with a fever. He read me W.C. Williams' *In The American Grain*, and I still remember the passage about Pocahantas and though I've read the book since, I remember him reading it to me. He was a great nurse, boy he loved it. Soup and flowers and William Carlos Williams, later Gertrude Stein. He laughed while he crossed his legs, as he sat in the chair, legs crossed, the book in his lap, both of us laughing, he could say the word wonderful. He put it there with us, at Black Mountain, he was an actor, and when he said isn't it wonderful his face was a stage, a terrific face, very mobile, very expressive. He was, of course, a first rate rat.

I stayed in bed for two weeks. After the first few days it wasn't fun any more, and I snapped at him. I felt like Alice. Alice unhappy.

"This fuckin' soup's COLD!"

He assumed an exaggerated hurt expression: eyes wide, eyebrows slanting up, lips trembling, voice rising:

"But but but I got it I mean it was hot when I got it —

I laughed, and he sat on the bed, dipped the spoon in the soup and brought it to my mouth. I lowered my eyes, the corners of my mouth went down, I looked at the spoon, and then at him: he had a tender-nurse expression. I said,

"What do you think I am?"

He smiled. "We know what you are, Fee, dear. Come come: eat."

"I don't want that shit," I said. "It's cold, and it's canned."

"Very well," he said, and ate my soup.

"Was it good?"

He looked at me.

"Chicken noodle is a favorite here."

"Terrific," I said.

Cigarette poised in his right hand, leaned his head back, closed his eyes, took a deep breath, lowered his head and leaned forward exhaling a kind of ecstatic whisper as he opened his eyes WIDE: isn't she *won*derful? Gertrude Stein.

Because I had poison ivy I couldn't play in the Student Faculty Turkeyday football game, another liberal left-over: the students needed me and I sat there on the sidelines watching: that fuckin' doctor said keep off yr feet etc. (Charley was in Yucatan), and because of a touchback — I can't remember who won! I think — in fact I think the faculty won! They had Bob Turner! The Potter! Did the faculty win? I think the students won because Jay scored the touchback! Afterwards, I asked for the ball, and as everyone left the field I stood up in stocking feet and tossed a pass to Duck, and then took a few steps, caught one and rifled it back. I was then carried back to bed, what a *bore!* poison ivy, ever since it's been a menace, always was, but when I was sitting on my bed after the game, and everybody else was in the Dininghall, I was so frustrated, I tore off my socks, the blisters had all gone flat.

The Serbian Dancer loved to dance: had danced in concerts with Merce and Katy at school, had rehearsed with them, and at the point where I got poison ivy, during the construction of the new Chem Lab, I heard that he had a heart attack while rehearsing, and the doctor told him he could never dance again. I can't tell you what it meant to him, and how it hurt him.

BLACK MOUNTAIN

The dirt road into the College began at the white fence, went by an empty wooden bungalow with a piano inside, passed between the softball field and the abandoned tennis court, rose up a slope to level off between the Dininghall, North Lodge and the Office, made a circle around the house where the woman I had a good thing going with lived: the dinner gong in her front yard (a three pole pyramid with an iron bar hanging). The road turned and passed the Quiet House — back in the trees ("A place for people to think or worship" the brochure said) passed the new Chem Lab and the Studies Building on a turn, and moved up the mountain passing wood and stone houses where faculty and married students lived. In heavy woods it curved over a couple of bridges and ended up on a rise to the farm. It was on this road, just below the Studies Building — under the Chem Lab, that M.C. decided we should have a game of poker. So we got table and chairs, the cards, some beer and got it going. The afternoon was sunny, and we were in good spirits, of course cars or trucks stopped, and angrily had to go, back down into and out of the circle, head down the road, leave the property, and on the asphalt road drive to the back road that led to the farm, another rocky road, but very spacious and country-like, with the farm always ahead in the distance. I walked it many times, to bring in stray cows. The Potshop was near there, just away from the island at the end of the lake, the cows liked it, push into the bushes and gaze into the Potshop at girls and boys throwing. Through a combination of openings between bushes and trees, and small clearings, like fields, we could see a corner of the Potshop clear across the lake from the Dininghall porch, and I remember one day at lunch Farmboy jumped up and yelled, THOSE GODDAMNED COWS! We looked, and there were three cows near the Potshop, making their way to the lake for a drink of polluted water and get stuck in the mud up to their chests. He ran out of the Dininghall, raced up the shortcut to the road, followed the road by the lake, went down the stone steps to the Library, through the tall grass at the foot of the Studies Building towards the Potshop where he intercepted the cows bouncing rocks off their skulls to our outcries, cheers and laughter, as distant to him as his snarling curses were to us. Alarmed, angry, and wounded, the cows lumbered back up the mountain to the farm. He returned, furious, glaring at us as we laughed.

DAYLIGHT SAVINGS

Every Saturday morning I rose to participate in the Work Program. Much more real than Liberal. It paid my way. I did a lot of different things. I kept the sewer lines open, had to send the wire snake up the pipe and fish from the far end, for globs of cotton soggy with piss and shit and blood and shreds of toilet paper. Remember the day after we had redbean soup? And the cesspool overflowed?

It was in a clearing in trees about fifty yards below South Lodge, near the houses where the cooks lived. I wore boots, didn't go barefoot. Piss and shit a pool in the grass around the tank, where Jack (Rice) and I stood.

"Okay," Jack grinned. "Let's look inside."

What a sight when we flipped the lid off! I turned away, face chalk white, tongue stuck out and eyes crossed, hands gripping my stomach. Jack laughed.

Well I also worked on the farm.

I also did road work. I also cut grass. I washed windows, swept, painted, scraped, fixed roofs, removed hot water heaters, collected stones, kept fires going, cut down trees — etc., and a problem developed there wasn't enough light to do all the work, which was too much anyway, hopeless. Black Mountain would never shape up. The kudzu weed. Dark green tendrils with big green leaves. The government had planted it all through the South to stop erosion, and some Liberal from the Forties thought it would stop the erosion down our mountain, so they planted it, not thinking ahead, and after they all left and Charley had the school, there was the kudzu weed — nothing can kill it: it grows anywhere. Moves fast, in its way. I know it's still there, sneaking down the mountain, across the road, over the house in the circle and across the path to the lake, remembering me. I cut a lot of kudzu weed. It grew about an eighth of an inch a day, or more, maybe a foot, and when it overran the house in the middle of the circle, the house looked like something out of a fairy tale: covered with giant, dark green ivy.

The school was broke, always. I don't think the faculty was paid the last year and a half I was there, and those last couple of winters were tough. There wasn't any coal, we built the coal bin for the Studies Building from stones on the mountain, and then there wasn't any coal to put in it. Sometimes it got bitter cold and when we got, on homebrew, so drunk — Dan and Cynthia and Tim and Jack and Victor and I — we huddled over a hotplate in Dan's apartment in the Studies Building, I, fireman — staggered downstairs, through the furnace room and outside, rooted around in the coal bin for a few bits for the hopper, and around four a.m. managed to stir up a little heat. Yet the homebrew, in the winter, kept on window ledges, was cold. Homebrew. Basil and Bert kept their crocks locked in an empty study until it was done, then sold it for twenty-five cents a quart. But Dan and I, using the knife trick Eric Weinberger taught us, slipped inside, dipped mason jars in the still bubbling brew, and back to my study. Remember the party when I drank homebrew from one of Katy Litz's galoshes? Christ it was awful stuff. Lou and Viola, or was it Jay? put orange slices, chunks of apples, and raisins in it, about a ten gallon crock: did I get stoned that night? *Me?* ...one of the faculty threw an easy chair through the plateglass window and ran out. We saw him running up the night mountain in shirtsleeves.

Two days later he showed up, freezing and wild eyed, staggered into the kitchen, tore a loaf of bread apart with his teeth and drank so much milk he got sick.

Several of us tried suicide, but it never worked. Sleeping pills, alcohol, drugs, auto accidents, etc., all planned, all deliberate, failed in strange and unexpected ways, and we are all alive.*

---

*Over twenty-five years later, with certain exceptions — Olson and Flola — it's still true. This footnote November, 1989. George, Joel and Robert Duncan died last year. Jim Herndon this year (1990).

We wrote stories, poems and plays, we drew, we painted, made sculpture, threw pots, danced, took photographs, composed and played music, had softball games in the summer and scratch football games in the winter and brought the cows in. And drank. The local tavern about four miles away, and we went there as often as we could to drink as much beer, they only had beer, as we could, and I got fat. The tavern closed at midnight, another hardship, infuriating me, so one afternoon, sitting on the steps to the Dininghall with Clark Kent — after I got out of the Army I got a postcard from sunny Florida, the creamily colored photo was of a Clark's Restaurant, located on some highway; the inked message read,

<blockquote>This is where Clark lives.
Love, Kitty</blockquote>

I knew Farmboy's handwriting. In or out of our camp.

We teased Clark pretty much, and though he was straight, he enjoyed it, and as he and I were friendly because we were midwestern types, we played catch together, etc., could communicate, to a point, and sitting on the steps to the Dininghall by the tree and the millstone, that day, I got the brilliant idea of how we could give two more daylight hours to the Work Program, which is how I proposed it to the faculty, during a meeting: I was an important member of the Work Committee, and I clinched it saying as we were outside of world time anyway, it didn't affect us, why not operate on our own schedules? Charley thought it was great, he loved to fuck up time, but Clark, who was also on the Work Committee, got excited — laughed and shouted, clapped his hands, did a dance because it meant we could stay at Peek's tavern until two in the morning.

Jack Rice, head of the Work Committee, of course saw through, we often got drunk together, he endorsed it. Other student and faculty members on the Committee also. My practical plan, and though there were objections from the cooks because of delivery schedules from outside, I reasoned if it was four to them and two to us, so what? They finally said okay, it was crazy but okay, and the faculty and student body likewise — all, in fact everybody but one.

The stubborn wife of Max Dehn insisted daylight saving time would interfere with Max's diet, and in no time she convinced other faculty members, and my grand plan was vetoed in the next faculty meeting.

Max died while I was in the Army. They buried him in the rhododendron below the reservoir.

I had never really known him, but we — I never took any of his classes — but we were friendly, always greeted each other, and occasionally stopped to talk a bit, on the road, or the path.

In his German accent, "How are you?" He had a little voice.

"Fine," I stammered, in awe of him.

He gazed up at me. "Are you writing, painting?"

I nodded. "I'm working on a book, and drawing, and doing caseins."

He became enthusiastic: his whole face brightened, took my arm — "Dot's good," he gravely said. "Dot's *good.*"

Just before I was drafted it was clear, though, that he was fading out.

He loved to walk in the woods and up the mountain. I see him walking through his life in physics in Europe and America, and at Black Mountain.

One cold misty autumn morning I was sitting on the boulders at the top of the mountain, gazing down the long field at my school in the valley, when I heard a muted rustle, and turning saw Max on the path among bushes and rocks and trees, by the barbed wire fence I'd helped string. I climbed down and we faced each other. His cheeks were drawn but pink: eyes deep and bright. White hair windblown, the collar of his jacket partly turned up. He was a little stooped. He smiled to me. I smiled hello, and murmuring hello in return, his bent little body shuffled past, and disappeared in the mist.

AT BOTTOM

I first read Melville's *The Confidence-Man* in 1951. Tough stuff. About a year later, it was easier. I enjoyed it a few years later, still an influence, a favorite book. *I like it.* On winter days and nights at Black Mountain, as I lay on my mattress in my study, reading at it again and again, making my way through, it showed me what I wanted.

Chapter 33, in the Grove Press paper edition, page 215, the chapter called *Which May Pass for whatever it May Prove to be Worth*, reads in part:
"But ere be given the rather grave story of Charlemont, a reply must in civility be made to a certain voice which methinks I heard, that, in view of past chapters, and more particularly the last, where certain antics appear, exclaims: How unreal all this is! Who did ever dress or act like your cosmopolitan? And who, it might be returned, did ever dress or act like harlequin?
"Strange, that in a work of amusement, this severe fidelity to real life should be exacted by anyone, who, by taking up such a work, sufficiently shows that he is not unwilling to drop real life, and turn, for a time, to something different. Yes, it is, indeed, strange that anyone should clamor for the thing he is weary of; that anyone, who, for any cause, finds real life dull, should yet demand of him who is to divert his attention from it, that he should be true to that dullness.
"There is another class, and with this class we side, who sit down to a work of amusement tolerantly as they sit at a play, and with much the same expectations and feelings. They look that fancy shall evoke scenes different from those of the same old crowd

round the custom-house counter, and same old dishes on the boarding-house table, with characters unlike those of the same old acquaintances they meet in the same old way every day in the same old street. And as, in real life, the properties will not allow people to act out themselves with that unreserve permitted to the stage; so, in books of fiction, they look not only for more entertainment, but at bottom, even for more reality, than real life itself can show. Thus they want novelty, they want nature, too; but nature unfettered, exhilarated, in effect, transformed. In this way of thinking, the people in a fiction, like the people in a play, must dress as nobody exactly dresses, talk as nobody exactly talks, act as nobody exactly acts. It is with fiction as with religion: it should present another world, and yet one to which we feel the tie."

The Confidence-Man, subtitled, *His Masquerade,* is a theater that liberates even the form of anecdotes. Melville's only dirty joke is in *The Confidence-Man:* it's his creative depiction of the white man's racist, two-faced doubletalk before the age of advertising: on a Mississippi Riverboat then, as streets nationwide today, where con men and beggars abound, and banks don't have signs with homilies regarding no trust — with puns on the word — but Have A Nice Day, instead.

DISHCREW

I hated dishcrew. It was hard dirty hot work, nothing good about doing it. *I hated it.* Who was that girl that yelled at me,
   "Well tough shit for you, Fee Dawson, you've GOT TO DO IT!"

FIRE AND LOVE

There weren't any grades at Black Mountain: classes, and particularly the language classes, moved fast, and though Flola didn't care if somebody didn't show up on Tuesday, when they came in on Wednesday they wouldn't know what anybody was talking about: her French class was two hours long, five days a week, and after the second day we spoke French, no English. She taught Spanish to Dan and Cynthia and Victor in just a few months so they could go to Mexico because they had seen *Viva Zapata!*

We had to go to classes or face the wrath of the teacher: there wasn't any kidding around. The other prevailing faculty attitude was if you missed class fuck you — classes were tough, we couldn't miss them — homework, heavy as it was, then doubled...it may have been free of academic rules and regulations, but that made it worse, the whole burden on us, and the faculty maybe getting plastered with us the night before no matter, we had to produce. To show up at Fiore's weekly painting seminars empty handed was embarrassing, in fact humiliating. I always had the feeling those Goddamned teachers waited for me, and more times than I can remember I slunk into Charley's class, or great Flola's French class, and the others, not having done the assignment, and because the classes were so small, God it was a nightmare, say when Charley asked me what I thought the crucial image in King Lear was and I hadn't read it (I did, it was the circle), but if I hadn't, and there were days I sat, eyes downcast, paralyzed as my fellow students gazed at me, and waited. Nobody said anything, and let me tell you, tension mounted. Charley got that sleepy look, and I said because I had to say something, I stuttered I didn't know, and he asked Nick, or Mike Rumaker, or Mark, or Mary, Harvey, etc., letting me sit in my stew, until he got something going. Lives changed in those classes, the competition was personal, and often my student friends said, after class, with a sideways glance and a murmur,

"You better quit fucking around and get to work."

Just as I said to them: we pointed fingers at each other, and the simplicity of language made reality spin. Dear Hitler.

"Where did Freud get his source material for Moses and Monotheism, do you think it's valid and why? — Fee."

He gave me his friendly dagger smile. I hadn't read the book. I said.

"I don't know where he got it, but it's probably valid."

He looked straight at me, still smiling,

"Did you read it?"

I lied, and said I began it, but didn't finish it.

"Don't lie to me!" he cried angrily. He leaned forward, saying,

"Do you know what I would do to you in *a real school?*"

I lowered my eyes and nodded.

"Yes," he said, "you do know. All right, next class you have a paper on the two questions I asked, otherwise you *flunk.*"

Flunk! What a terrible word at Black Mountain! Charley used it with a pointed finger at the end of a long arm, eyes blazing,

"*You flunk.*"

I went over to Hitler while he was having coffee, after supper, in the Dininghall. I sat next to him.

"Listen," I pleaded, "I can't write that paper — "

He looked surprised. "Paper?"

I know my face darkened, and he laughed.

"I hate that fuckin' book, I can't read it! *You* know! It's *impossible!*"

He nodded.

Man, that was a weird school. I read the book and wrote a rotten paper.

The graduation process was too complicated to remember, and it did change, or, well, nobody wanted to graduate anyway... Phyllis,

Jorge, Peter, Trueman, and Mark are the only ones I can recall. I decided not to, but I had considered it. I would have had to spend my last year reviewing, in full, all the subjects I had taken in the first three years, which meant French. Flola knew why I decided against graduating. Yet — I knew I had one year at maximum before going into the Army, and I didn't want to spend it reviewing what I had done. I wanted to write, paint and draw — I used to stand outside Mike Rumaker's study and listen to him type. That guy *wrote*. Clickety click clack click into the wee hours on his big L.C. Smith typewriter.

There were more steps to graduating. After I had reviewed my first three years, I would be subject to cross examination by the students, and then, with only the Student Moderator (Dan) present, by the faculty. The Student Moderator had the capacity to tell the faculty they were being too tough. It was like a trial. The next and last step was an examination by any person in the world involved in the particular field. I wanted to graduate because I wanted W.C. Williams to come down and be my Examiner. Franz came down for Jorge, and Paul Goodman came down for Mark.

Black Mountain was not an accredited school — eighty-six across the nation, but the people who did graduate, mostly in the old days, were quickly snapped up by the Ivy League schools, or more Liberal departments in large universities.

The graduation certificate home made. Lettered by hand, a beautiful document, and we all stood around and smiled, and then got wasted.

She walked out of the Studies Building, I beside *her*. *She* said,
"Don't follow me."
"I love you."
Just beyond the light from the doorway, *she* turned, and glared at me,
"No you don't. It's yourself. Can't you see that?"
She disappeared in darkness. I ran after, calling,

"It isn't! It's you — CAN'T YOU SEE IT'S YOU?"
Her voice came back,
"No — all I hear is you. I keep hearing you. You'll find out."
"Is that a threat?"
Soft steps receded. I heard a distant response — "No."
"I do love you."

Nothing.

I turned, began back towards my study, but then turned again, and walked down to the Dininghall, wanting to — not knowing what to do — walk, wondering why I was ALWAYS impotent, wondering if it would *ever* end.

The next morning before breakfast, in front of the Dininghall, two students had a fist fight over a girl.

I watched them sit, separately, at tables: one boy wept.

The Mailbox used to be inside the doorway of the Studies Building, and one day Charley was standing there with a book in his hand.

As I passed him, he yelled to me,

"THOSE SONS OF BITCHES — THEY STOLE MY WORD!"

Projection. Boy, *that* turned me around.

While I was in the Army John and Elaine Chamberlain were there, and John tells the story of Elaine in right field picking flowers, while Jonathan Williams, on each at bat, hit five high drives to right field, and she glanced up, saw the ball in the air, left her flowers, and caught it.

None of us, ever wore dark glasses, Except Jay.

Stan Vanderbeek lettered like a master.

I wrote my mother how Ed Dorn leaped up and down steps.

One evening men from the mountain across the valley came saying there was a forest fire: it had started in Kentucky, come down through Tennessee into the Carolinas: volunteers sought, and of course, some of us went, and when we got to the mountain, across the valley, that night, watching the small flames move towards us — the flames that ate leaves, twigs and bushes in advance of the wall of fire — the state trooper conservationist chose captains, and running his eyes over our faces, he chose me. So I had command over about six of us in the work of clearing a wide swath...reminding me of the drawing class I taught, and the trouble I had with a student who would not listen, he had to draw lines over the lines over the lines over the line he had first drawn — couldn't leave it alone. On the mountain that night, J.P. Grady and I got lost: our flashlight batteries wore out, and we walked down, into the valley, and a gully in terrific darkness, finally arrived at the appointed cabin: the Black Mountain gang had gone — where had we been? the farmer asked. Lost, we said.

Spring, 1950
    Charley stood on a street in bright daylight. Washington, D.C. Something was in the air. He looked up.
    Saw a Soviet bomber in the sky. Stared at it in a gathering anxiety and fascination. It held the Bomb.
    He woke, frightened.
    Told us that morning, on the porch, spellbound, looking out over the lake, astonished eyes drilled into space. What did it mean?

He had left politics around 1944 to write for keeps. I think it was 1945 when Caresse Crosby published *Y & X*. *Call Me Ishmael*, which he began, as it happened, the day FDR died, and ended the morning of Hiroshima, formed an exit from politics to the influence of Pound, and created the entrance into his personal poetic experience. Reynal & Hitchcock published the book in 1947, and later, at Black Mountain, Albers read it, liked it, and invited Charley down to lecture on Melville. (Not true. Albers had invited Dahlberg, who couldn't go. Olson took Dahlberg's place.) Charley went, and was a success. Albers invited him for the summer (1949).

But a political crisis was taking place in the school — I don't know about it at all, it's hard for me to remember the battles for power, so many of the teachers were fathers to me, especially Charley, I was young, too young, too sensitive to sharp-tongued older students, and adult anger, as later when Charley and the farmer Doyle came to hate each other. Charley for History and Art. Doyle with Natasha and Bill Levi for Science. Very difficult for me. I liked Doyle, he and I had worked hard together, many a night it was the two of us that finished the job and put the tools away, after twelve and fifteen hours.

In June of 1949 Albers and the classical figures behind Black Mountain left. I never met them. I arrived a month later, in July. Buckminster Fuller was there with his group from Chicago. I liked Fuller. I had never met anyone like him. Or anyone like Charley, or Vashi, and of course Arnold, Joe and Herndon, Hank, (boy there were some real bastards, too: that guy with the green prescription glasses...) my turning nineteen that summer was a drag.

So going into the fall of 1949, to me it was Charley's school, Bill Levi didn't think so, neither did Natasha, philosophy and science, with hands hardly "bloodstained from the slaughter of a thousand platitudes," as Ortega puts it, in *The Revolt of the Masses*...but it was Charley's. He envisioned a commitment of his own making — his creative ego — it paid off immediately: he got a second Guggenheim for research in Yucatan, and like a man liberated, Charley wrote, and talked — he wrote with such intensity his ideas — if he thought it, it appeared on paper.

But starting in 1950, Wes and M.C., and Hazel, Flola, Natasha, Joe, Bill, all fighting among themselves, managed to keep the school — dare I say it! — going for Charley while he was away, because when he came back, he returned to his own, brimful of fire...

He had written the Essay on Projective Verse in 1950.

Right around then he had the dream.

It was as if he had left politics and Pound and headed towards himself in History and Art and Black Mountain.

We were right there with him.

The point, the trigger, the moment of change occurred from about August 1949 to the fall of 1951: the *Essay*, the handset edition of *Appolonius of Tyana, Letter to Melville*, the correspondence with Creeley, *The Mayan Letters*, the beginning of Corman's magazine *Origin*, dozens and dozens of excellent poems, voracious reading (he reads let me tell you, Charley reads, and we felt it — listen, listen to M.C. Listen to Dierkes, listen to me, Charley was possessed by his voice and History [one of my real regrets is missing the class he gave, How to Read a Newspaper. 1954. I was in the Army.]). Charley was red hot, and Black Mountain rose into a tower of realized force of us at work.

In a developed, cultured and keen consciousness, snakes, spiders, insects, etc., are still imbued with the dark and archaic symbolism of a lethal death-touch, almost magic, the terror of contact. And a well polished, smooth running complicated machine holds a psychic glitter — symbolizing the latest technological form of a deadly creativity, magical enough to cast a spell...a shining surface imbued with a killing force.

Charley's dream, an anxiety dream, foretold his future.

He had written Nick and I a letter from Yucatan, in 1951, which reads in full:

> fieldingnick:
> if the lost art of stealing bases

                    maketh the finest play, noh you
                    how man is new, is no
                    paul,
                    or christ?
                                        his average was low
                                who said: if i am not the christ
                                it is a disagreeable
                                mistake
                                but if man sheds
                    such white sox, then
                    does he lead the league by paul?
                                o, save us from all spectators & humanists:
            shall we not take any man down gently or otherwise?
                                who'll buy
                this franchise? will you or you? (here's rue or guanabana
                            for he who has
                            taste
agri, dulce y amarga
donde el llega
al pleno
dominio
de su arte
                                        art
                                        is the twin of
                                        the game: how
                                        do you dance, now
                                        base-stealers?

(straight translation
from the Three Eye
to you, to
the top!)
                            And this one walked from one
                                end of the field
                            (the old field, Commisky Park,
                                the Indians
                            Di Mag) to the other, to where
                            the Atlantic is, looking

> for local gods. And finding
> (solamente)
> himself

July, 1949.

On the train to Black Mountain (it was my first Pullman ride), I was looking out the window, slightly hypnotized in almost empty, well-cushioned car, an air slowed. Serene. Warm. And as in haze —
"*You are going to a place and you will change.*"
I — panicked, how I feared that voice! Yet I — I wanted it, I rushed to it, running, and when I read,

"What does not change / is the will to change"

I knew I had found the guy.

Here are some of my notes taken in Charley's classes (this book is his).

"Mechanical — better word than contrived — for Faulkner"
 "Francis Parkman—LaSalle or The Discovery of the Great West"
 "Melville who writes not to tell the truth but to give the evidences"
 "Converts sea to land — who knows farming — and the combination" — !!! *terrific* — "increases his force and making it available to anyone — brought the sea home — Homer keeps all action on the *skirt* — the edge — of land and sea — Moby Dick an act of farming — an act of industry.
 "Taking experience and making it into image"
 "Poe and Melville's language essentially English

— W.C. Williams' prose stems from Poe"
"Parkman 23 when he wrote The Oregon Trail
Melville 25 typee pub same time"
"Ingersoll & the pamphleteers sources of Pound's prose — much like American advertising — problem not to write — but to *present* — act of energizing a given field — "
"Lawrence's prose American"
"Carlisle false thing on Melville — Pierre — passage where he finds pamphlet on coach — Christ time & man time — "

"The Bomb blasted history."
Thursday, Sept 27, 1951

"Mycene
   7 cities of Troy
   Schlemann Troy 1875
   Evans Crete — 1905
   ?
Assyrian — 5000 BC
   Gladwin — Men out of Asia
Owen Lattimore — inner frontier of Eastern Asia
   35,000 BC limits indus East W. Calif coast
   5,000 BC 1st city URUK (mesopatamia)
   SPACE

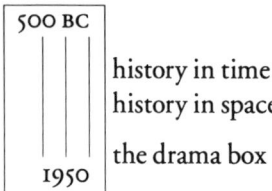

history in time
history in space
the drama box

Jane Harrison — 1900-5-1910 Ancient Art & Ritual
                                              basic stuff
Prologomena to the study of Greek Ritual (1905)

have worked from   Priapus — Richard Payne
   404 BC   Knight
1951 — on same   picks up where
basic plane —   Harrison leaves off"
& BMC has gone on
from that point

Thurs, Apr 4 52
"Sociology — Human Ancest — Artemus Gates on Eskimo (1910)
R.H. Factor (S. American — William Boyd)
Carl O. Sauer (Environment & culture in the Deslaciation)
Proceeding on American Philogical Society — 1947"
(What is the matter with Mary tonight. Joe is mad because he had a fight with Olson at the Summer Sessions meeting over Tworkov — I love Joe and I love Mary — but together they're different — they love me too — this looks lousy written like that — this. Vacation in 2 days — I don't want to go home. I will though.)

"Frobenius: diffusion into Spain from Afrik
Herodotus
  &
Gates   HAWKES
  &
Rhys Carpenter"
"The philosophy of language is inseparable to Archaeology"

"Always engage yrself to the point of highest intensity"

Monday May 27 1952
"Time is broken open — History is dead — time in terms of man is space — space is instantaneous — true of time too — time now is not history

no novel/no short story/no climax   it's
busted up, that's why
Toynbee — Huge Christian journalist
reinforce Henry Luce

Dawn   Dreiser"
Newspaper days

May 15 Thursday 1952
"Prose verb
_____
Verse — noun"
"PAST IS PRESENT AT MOMENT OF WRITING"
Time as tense is the verbal force"
"If the subject is worth anything it should change the object"

Monday night May 19, 1952

"You love people without ever having seen them — & that is a tremendous truth."

"Mystery is not mysterious — it is the fact of life"

"reach this plane — image & rhythm you use to get there — before though, you must *recognize* — "

"The sun & the flesh — "

"credo in Una   feminine accusative
I believe in God   making God the father
                     a goddess"
"'I want to get to the other side of despair.' — Rimbaud"

"Herodotus treats events as *around* — he casts no shadow —

the event leaves neither forward nor backward — the American faces past event as he faces present action — "

"To work on the present — the present holds the action — Herodotus presents his events instantaneously —

"Hitler was the death of Europe — Europe could not be looked upon as a man — "

"LOVE IS A VERB"

"Why make a simile when you can make a metaphor."
"Metaphor nothing to do with comparison — it's recognition."
"Kitasono — the rhythm of the man."

"The moving function is the verb. Write your own sentence! The character of the 19th Century is its descriptive power."

Thurs. May 20, 1952.
'Milton perverses the language to go along with classical form.'"
— W.C.W.
"In every aspect I think Milton is a second rate mind. Milton needs to be taken apart as a thinker — in his philosophy and his theology."

"Art today is a moral act."

"You cannot deny life. It demands from you — & when you *answer* those demands — THERE is the rhythm."
"The filth is in the withdrawal."
"Recite poetry — at the highest pitch."
"The American language is a Goddamned subtle instrument."

"Let 'em (the Reds) come — I'm busy."

(1938   Dear Fielding, my boy:

I guess you have been having a pretty good time the last few weeks, with Christmas, and your sister Cara's birthday and Valentine's Day, — and now next Wednesday is Washington's Birthday. It just seems that life is just one good time after another, doesn't it.

Won't it be nice when we all get together again? You and Cara and mother and me. I think that will be pretty fine, — and when I can come to your birthday parties and things. And when we can have another good old game of Wolf Kazan. Do you remember? Oh, boy.

And when we do get together again, I hope it will be here in New York, because there are a lot of things here that I want to show you. I'd like to show you the Empire State Building, Rockefeller Center and Radio City, — and of course, next summer the World's Fair will be here in New York.

And then sometime I'd take you down to the Battery to see the big boats come in from across the Atlantic Ocean, — England, and France and Italy, and all sorts of places. And we'd stand there on the Breakwater and look out over New York Harbor and see the Statue of Liberty, and Brooklyn Bridge, — but maybe we wouldn't see any big boats, — only coal barges and ferry boats. So I'd probably turn to a policeman and say, "Officer," I'd say, kind of polite because he's a policeman, "When are the big boats due?" "Well," he'd say, and he'd rub his chin, because he can think better when he rubs his chin, "Well," he'd say, "the Normandie is due at 4:30, and the Aquitania at six o'clock, but — " and then he'd brighten up, "if you'll come back next Tuesday, the Queen Mary will be coming in." "O.K.," we'd say, "Thanks."

Then I'd turn to you and I'd say, "Fielding, my boy," I'd say, — just kind of man-to-man like, "the Normandie comes in at 4:30 and it's only 2:30 now. Suppose we go over to the Aquarium and see the fish while we're waiting." "O.K., Dad," you'd say, "That's a good idea." "All right," I'd say, "Let's go, – – – – – – – but wait a minute. We want to see the fish, and I suppose the fish want to see us, but I feel kind of hungry. And I suppose the fish would like to see us looking happy and well-fed. I think maybe we should have something to eat. I wouldn't want the fish to look out of their tanks and think, 'Just look at that poor man and that little fellow. They look so hungry and half starved' — I think maybe we should have a hamburg sandwich before we went in." "Well, Dad," you'd say, "I think I could handle a hamburger pretty well." "O.K.," I'd say, "will you have relish or onions?" "Relish," you'd probably say. "All right," I'd say, "I'll have onions and lots of mustard."

Well, I hope things turn out that way, because I know we'd enjoy it, — mother and Cara and you and me. We'd all have a good time, and we could have all of your aunts and uncles and friends come to visit us. If we all got together here in New York, you could write back to all of your friends and say, "Dear Billy" (or "Dear Susie" or "Dear Jimmy") — "If you come to the World's Fair in New York, I hope you will come and see me. I live at 123 So-and-So Street."

And now lots of love to you all. Kiss Cara for me, and mother, and kiss all of your aunts, — but just shake hands with Essex, because he's a man, and men don't kiss. They do in France, but it looks kind of funny. I suppose mother is back in Kirkwood now, and I guess you were pretty glad to have her come back. You can kiss her twice for me.

With lots of love.
   Dad)

We had never met anyone like Franz.

When Dan introduced me, in the kitchen that evening of Franz's second day — I think (I rather avoided him before, wanted to look at him, a little), when Franz and I shook hands I knew by the warmth in his eyes and hand, he must have felt my reciprocal gesture, too, meeting a man I had never met before. Strange that — years later I was startled, and awed that Franz introduced me to Ornette Coleman in the same way.

I see the plural we above. The regulars were so entrenched in Black Mountain, it was our identity, by then, and when Franz brought his world into ours, the similarity was fantastic. Here from the Outside, an Inside man! Much like ourselves, yet quite unlike us. His world was streets, his loft, his art, his life. In our militant-artistic yet spiritual alienation, Franz appeared to stimulate us. Meaning I had a chance, which is why I laughed so that night in the Cedar when he called Black Mountain downtown Manhattan, again including it in his experience. I was made proud because I had been there, thus in his experience.

But the price of it was Franz's rejection of Charley, and who knew why? Because Charley towered over him and talked the way that only Charley could? Because Charley had brought Franz into his, Charley's thought? Because Charley, in his perception and deduction had included Franz even before Franz had arrived? It makes sense.

In the way he signed his letters, the double k meant kee klops, or cyclops, Charley was — in all reading of Carlos Williams, Pound and Homer, he was, affectionately, our Cyclops: behind his back we made jokes about him and whales: he didn't like that.

Charley very serious about whales.

Once, after he had talked about Roosevelt's charm, he was surprised when I said,

"That's what killed him."

He looked at me, astonished. "By God, that's right!"

The identifying brilliance, wit, charm, and sensitivity that reveals religion, childhood emotions and reflects a secret guilt found in the titles of Franz's paintings, is in Charley's Maximus Letters — the religious passage when Charley meets the priest on the hometown street. Somehow to a point that both men, at bottom, relate to religion. And childhood.

A big poet, a smaller artist: opposites with like values, well, no wonder it didn't work. Both revealing themselves in talk. If you want to understand Charley's poems, he's talking. Franz too.

But Franz rejected him. Asked him how old he was.

"Forty one."

Franz condescending,

"I'm older than you are." Franz smug.

Charley — stared at Franz. We were on the steps to the Dininghall, by the tree, the bench and the millstone — Charley hurt, as if saying, "But Franz, this isn't what I — this isn't IT!"

Years and years after, I fought a war to get them into my heart in the realization that my love was not a division of myself, but two single, separate, isolated, emotions. For you, Franz. For you, Charley. As real as my love for my original father.

(1940 typewritten: Dear pop,
   How are you? I hope you are fine. I have been playing basketball over at Hobey's house. It's lots of fun, especially where there are about five people to each side. I've picked up some jokes heare and their, so here they are —
   Abott & Costello were walking along the street and Costello said "Abott what are those men doing?" (they were building a ship) And Abott said thats a hull of a ship (say that fast) Costello, I know but what are those men doing.   ?

   Costello, Abott where do all the little bugs go in the winter? Abott, search me. Costello, No thanks I just wanted to know.

   The judge walks into the court, sits down, and pounds on the stand, and yells ORDER ORDER ORDER. A man in the back yells I'll take Pepsi-cola.

   Dad it's too bad we can't have any popcorn...do you know why? Because all the colonels are in the army.

   Well I have to leave you now.
                              Goodbye
   P.S. Lots of love
   OoOoOoOoOoOoOoOoOoOoOoOoOo
   these things stand for love
                              Fielding)

Because Dan and I had been to Black Mountain together, and because Franz had liked us and the school immediately, and later came to love it, and because Dan and I stayed close to Franz, very close, until he died, it is part of Black Mountain's effect on us, as we were together, that we experienced Franz as we did.

There was a way he stood at the bar, in the Cedar, and because of the character of light that came in the front window, and struck Franz, there was a way the glass of beer in his hand became a crystal twinkle, and when he drank it, put it down, murmured satisfaction, sucked foam from his lips, turned, winked and said,

"*Boy!* The first one's *always* the best."

A design came into view.

The bar — the rows of bottles, Louie in his clean white apron, the front window, the sparkling beertaps — came into focus, and from out of each thing's mystery, voices came, the glass had a message and the wooden bar was important: Franz was the medium, to me.

In 1958 Gil Sorrentino lived in Flatbush and he and I edited a little pamphlet called NEON: SUPPLEMENT TO NOW.

I gave Franz a copy; it was a beautiful little publication that led off with the birthday poem Charley had written to me at Black Mountain in 1951...

>   pitcher, how
>   exactly is
>   the feeling of the threads
>   what it is — that is,
>   the drama we know about,
>   the g(love)
>
>   or how is bush league bush
>   (man) made major, made
>   to bear in, to bear
>   down? in what sense is
>   to hit long before the ball
>   reaches
>   whoever?
>
>   where does giddiness

>   where is it
>   ceased — how can you say how
>   you can be said to be
>   cool, can throw it
>   exactly as how the ball is, how
>   you be sd to hurl?
>
>   (again): the whirl
>   is very much exaggerated, the
>   crowd, the afternoon, and, even,
>   the exhilaration of the home
>   run, though the centerfield wall
>   — to point at it — is exactly
>
> a like term, is also
> as you pitch
>
> that is, as of a day, a
> double day, say, as this, when
> there is a crowd, how would you say
> how far back you are reaching from,
> say, big train, from, the dirt, in what way
> do you obey
> the given, the
> taken — how much grip
> do your fingers have
> on those threads, or
> for that matter,
> the hide, eh?

Jonathan Williams had a poem in the pamphlet, Max Finstein had two, Creeley two, Gil had two, and there were two prose pieces, one by Selby, and one by me; when I gave it to Franz, I fairly blushed with pride.

He thanked me and that was the end of it.

My disappointment and hurt was nothing new to him. Once I had written a really lovely one page story and had it framed, and

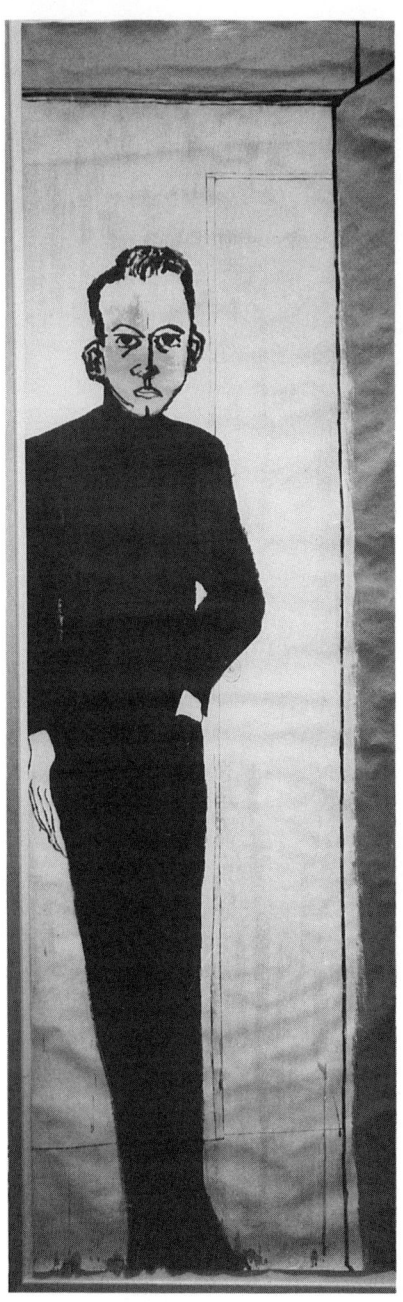

JONATHAN WILLIAMS
(F.D., 1951, Casein on Butcher Paper, Photograph by Mimi Fronczak)

gave it to Franz for Christmas. I saw it by chance years later on the floor with some junk in the back of his closet.

(1941 Dear Dad,
I hope I can come out to the hospital and see you Sunday. Mom doesn't know I'm writing this letter. I'm doing pretty good in school in arithmetic I get 90s or 80s in arithmetic. Hobey's sister Jeane has got a horse and 3 dogs and about 6 guniea pigs. They named the horse Donny. At first I was a bit afraid of the horse but today I got a ride on it and it was a bit scary at first but after a while its not so bad but its lots more fun than I thought it was going to be. I wanted to go to the show tonight but mom won't let me go. Last night Uncle Essex took 3 flashbulbs pictures of me flash bulbs are the kind of bulbs Newspaper photographers use I was sossposed to be a spook or gost. He fixed a sheet over my head and put a mask on me and I really did look like a spook. He said I was the only real spook in history. That mit you gave me sure is a good one I don't know what Id do if it wasn't for that glove. That glove is so good all the kids beg to use it
   Singing off
    Fee
P.S. Dont forget to answer me and you write a letter to me)

At Black Mountain it was a rule not to bother Charley: a rule like a law. I obeyed.

There's Black Mountain students that are embittered, and rightly so, and there's them that want to remember, and them that want to forget, and them that don't care. But no matter, Black Mountain worked: it was real, we made a potent little mandala in an archaic valley in the Blueridge Mountains to be felt *long* into the future.

I checked out the Horned Beetle: it's a Stag Beetle, but it isn't the same, proving what Charley always felt, that our valley was original: the beetle we saw was older, it had a hump and its body was longer, broader: Stag its later child.

Often when I walked down the road from the Studies Building, at night, with the distant light on the pole ahead — where the path to the Dininghall intersected the road — often the pole light was out — I would pause in the darkness, my bare feet almost feeling the touch of snakes. The darkness of cloudy moonless Carolina nights was so dense it was as if it was behind vision, my hands were out before me, standing there, I felt within the brute power of the mountain, the dark lake and the stillness — the stillness within, which frightened, yet astonished me, and I slowly gave in to it, to receive darkness within the darkness of an archaic gulf, the devastating *feel* of a primal valley fed by creeks and rivers come down a black mountain from a dark galaxy: I listened, feeling it all, deep in the slow stirring rock beneath my feet expressed in the softest night moisture on my half naked body, and the vast still threshold of the universe at my fingertips, against the base of the reservoir of my skull.

A slender pink and white girl with red hair showed up six weeks late, in the fall of 1951. She wore a freshly starched red and white small-checked shirt, with tail out, button down collar: clean white pants, white sneakers. The shirt hung straight down. Her hair coppery red, and brushed back around the ears like a city boy's. Shirt unbuttoned three down.

She smoked filter tipped cigarettes: used a Ronson lighter. Had nice lips, sensitive, and of course I had shown enough people around to know she was apprehensive of the place, and me showing her around (the routine), and defensive about being new. She smoked like a man, yet as her arms were so slender, a femininity came through. Her hand trembled a little as she puffed.

Her face was flat, so well scrubbed it glistened. Her eyes cool.

She was tense, so we paused on the rising curve of the road to the Studies Building, and she gazed out over the lake and valley.

"Gee," she said, "it's beautiful."

With an impatient gesture flipped her cigarette into tall grass, glanced at me bitterly.

"Been here long?"

"Two years."

"Is that long?"

I grinned and she smiled. "That's long," I said. "It'll be longer."

"You like it."

We began to walk. "I love it."

I showed her around the Studies Building...there were so few students she could have just about any study she wanted. We walked up and down the top and bottom corridors, occasionally meeting students. I introduced her — always good to have a new girl arrive, and this one, slender, very American looking, different, was welcome, yes, and though I did sense, that first day some of what it was, it was only later that it all came into focus.

I looked down into the opening of her shirt and saw she didn't have a bra on. I was shocked, and pleased. She liked.

I showed her the farm, and we walked back down to the lodges. On the way she asked what I did. I told her, and then asked her, although I knew she was a writer (her application).

"I'm a writer," she said.

"Hum," I nodded. "What are you working on?"

"A novel."

"What about?"

"A girl I knew."

"Knew?"

She looked at me pointedly. "She's dead."

I didn't quite know what to make of that — we walked in silence.

"I'm sorry," she said.

I nodded, wondering.

"It's too soon," she said. "I'll tell you about it again. Some time."

I told her when supper was served and said so long. She smiled thanks, and went up the steps into North Lodge.

I went to the Dininghall, got a cup of coffee, looked at the clock on the stove, the only clock around, nobody ever knew what time it was, and went out on the porch to think about the new girl.

M.C. was there, having tea and reading from Ulysses. Her class would begin in a half an hour. She didn't want to be disturbed. But saw I was glad to see her — she had introduced me to the new girl and asked me to show her around.

I sat across the table from her, tilted my chair, rolled up a smoke and tried to think.

M.C., with a low laugh, in a grave, basso Judge Reilly voice, said, "Well, Fielding. It's clear you want to talk."

She changed her voice to M.C. friendly. "What do you think of the new girl?" She paused, and like a lady lawyer, "Isn't that what you want me to ask?"

I laughed yes. "She's — interesting. I think she's gay."

"Does that make her interesting?"

I felt defensive, and couldn't answer. M.C. said,

"Don't you think it's because she's so new?"

"Yes," I admitted. My hand, not visibly, was trembling like the new girl's, and M.C. knew it. So, tactfully, she asked,

"Have you read the chapters for today?"

"Yes, for the second time," *I had read Ulysses.*

"Okay," she said, rising, "I'm going over now and make some *espresso* for us. See you."

She said espresso with a flair and I laughed. Later I went to class. I remember Alex there, and Cicely: were Pat and Russell?

At supper I sat with the new girl, and that night she chose a study. I helped her move her stuff in: later, as somebody made a beer run, we chipped in, and went to my study and listened to records and talked.

A knock on the door, and it was Tim, who came in smiling, with three cans of beer in his hand. He scratched his head, and glanced at the floor.

"I've brought three cans of beer," he said.

Another knock on the door. Victor.

"Behold!" he cried, stumbling backwards into the hallway—"a lady!"

The studies were small, and it got smoky. I opened a window, and we talked and read each other poems and told stories: we ran out of beer. Very depressing. We stole some wine, drank some of the dregs of the homebrew, went down to the Dininghall for peanut butter sandwiches, and then to bed.

The next day, she asked me,
"Did you ever read *Nightwood?*"
I shook my head.
"You ought to," she said.
"Is it good?"
She nodded. "It's my favorite book."

She wore a heavy ID bracelet, which she slid up and down her forearm. I asked her if she had ever read William Carlos Williams and she said the only Williams she'd ever read was Tennessee. I said he was the wrong one, she ought to read Doctor Williams, and I mentioned Charley, Pound, Frobenius, etc.

"Yeah," she exhaled. "Maybe I will."

She later changed the lives of two girls there, one, from a defensive plump pink faced girl who loved Eddie Fisher and Ted Williams into a hard talking gun carrying Miami lady cop whom I later saw in a bar in the Village. I asked her how she felt about Ted Williams — me with my smile — and she sneered, showing teeth, mentioning she'd seen him in a Miami hotel, said something about a first class bastard, made a brief karate chop in the air of farewell, and joined a couple of hard-eyed bulls in a dark corner. Gay bars were dark then.

The other girl she helped switch, was shy, short, very slender with hollow eyes, hollow cheeks and shoulders thrust forward: innocent enough, smart too, and later icy, bitter, and though I haven't seen her in years, my memory of her on a street in New York, of her laconic snort, with twisted lips, upon the mention of Black Mountain — and the sharp gleam of pain in her black eyes, does remind me of the effect of my scrubbed white faced red haired Lesbian, whom I at last made love to. Most of us wrote about her — having been affected...her telling that international story naming famous names and blue lit places in her past, and of the strange rich seventeen year old girl who committed suicide.

This was all on the heels of the days with Kitty, Hitler, and Dancer! they were gone, all away. Farmboy left, but he came back, and later he left for good. We five had made a pact.

At night, in the Studies Building; sitting Indian style on the hallway floor, just outside the door to my study. The pledge was we would never forget, and as I sterilized the razor blade with a match, they held out their thumbs. I made a small incision in my thumb, sucked it, as they, Kitty, Hitler, Farmboy and Dancer, did likewise. We then connected our thumbs in the air, and as we bled, vowed,

"I Fee, will never forget."

In blood: we kissed, and broke up because there were classes to go to.

In September of 1952 Dan and I began work on the superstructure of the Tobacco Barn.

The bare concrete foundation in the grass, in the Lower Pasture on the mountain side, out there in the open, startled me, but its effect, or my response illustrates the character of Black Mountain humor, the empirical perception articulated. A thing, upon sight, was something of speech. As a dog, upon seeing a bone,

"A bone!"

We thus isolated and crystalized metaphors, which was why, at twenty-one, I was able to open a story with a first line,

"Monday is a metaphor."

(The alliteration amused me.)

The fact that a metaphor existed, I mean that something was called a different name to represent what it was, was, to me, amazing.

If someone used a metaphor, it was natural for one of us to remark that that was a metaphor. A metaphor was as clear as a potato. Because of the potato. Our unveiled simplicity was easy to mock.

When a middle aged little student named Speedy, who was anything but, wrote his poem about the lake, and called it, mistakenly, *a mirrow*, we — all of us — plus and especially Charley, were taken. The misspelling was accepted, the word became a fact.

"LOOK AT THAT!" Charley yelled. "LOOK AT THAT GODDAMNED *WORD!*"

Dan and I walked up beyond the barn.
He said, "It's just ahead."
We veered out into the rising field, passing cows and chickens. Dan pointed. I saw the concrete foundation.
"That's it," he chuckled.
"It sure is real," I murmured.
"Well, let's get started."

About twenty by one hundred feet: the wood we were to use was rough hewn oak cut from mountain trees. We had two hammers, a small level, a saw and a keg of 20-penny nails. No ladders. The first thing we did was to select the straightest round poles for the uprights, each being about six inches in diameter and about seven or eight feet tall, make sure of their same length, and measure and mark off the spacing between each upright: we put around ten poles on the sides, and four across at each end, including corner poles.

The concrete foundation had a thick slab of oak bolted on for a sill, clear around, and the way we got the heavy vertical poles up was, by taking turns, toeing the nails at the base of each, holding it in place while either Dan or I went up the Pasture and looked down:
"To your right — a little left — okay."

Dan hit the nails, on each side of the base of the pole, down in at V-angles, and before he made the final blows, looked up at me. I again called directions.

He drove the nails in, and if we thought that was hard work, which it was, it was peanuts to what came later: this was *oak*.

A 20-penny nail is at least five inches long: unless driven in correctly was useless, and to toe that nail in one of those poles was almost impossible. Oak is the toughest wood there is, so what if I'm wrong. It won't give, it's bulky, each fibre affixed to the next in a dense grain. Oak doesn't break. It isn't resilient…if a nail is hammered a quarter of an inch into oak it is a quarter of an inch into oak, because what will happen a quarter of an inch later is not guaranteed by the quarter of an inch before: nails on their way into oak aren't carried forward by the depth of their shaft in the wood, as in that rather Protestant soft sweet smelling white pine. Oak is brute will. The single determining factor in the nail progressing into oak is the workman's eye, and hammer. No workman la dee da gets a nail into oak: oak demands the fusion of power and concentration, nobody is humming or whistling while nailing into oak, and because its surface is no less obdurate than its center, and vice versa, the task from beginning to end is a sequence of exact arm swings, and after the first nail is in, it is with a sinking of the heart that the workman picks up the next to do it again, to yet do it again — oak defies the pleasure of getting the job done. Through perfect concentration on the nailhead: there's no thinking. The mind no help with oak. Only the eye, arm, hammer and nailhead. The work goes slow.

My initial experience with oak, that first day, was a crashing realization of the job ahead. I held the large pole on an angle, and tried to get the 20-penny nail in — just to start it. My arm, my wrist, my shoulder — I was a helpless failure, and I looked up at Dan, my eyes wide and frightened —

"Dan! It just — won't — I can't get the nails in!"

He looked at me, and nodded. "That's oak."

I threw the pole on the ground, turned and gazed at the open foundation, and the pile of heavy poles, and rough one by five inch planks —

"Do you mean — we're going to have to — build this WHOLE *BUILDING* WITH IT?"

"It's the only wood we have."

I sat down staring at the lumber, the keg of nails, feeling rage — Dan was getting this side of nowhere with the toeing in, and while I hated Black Mountain for being so broke it couldn't buy wood, I also a little hated Dan because he had worked with oak before. Why hadn't someone told me? Why hadn't Dan warned me? I looked at him dripping sweat, bending and driving those nails from his heels. DiMaggio, Ted Williams — NEVER swung with such concentration. And the wonderful sound, so seldom heard: that small, profound deep-pitched click coming up through the nail shaft into the head of the hammer, into the hand up through the arm: a clean hit, which sharpened the eye that much more. That came later for me.

I gazed down the Pasture. I saw the farm: glinting white corner of the Studies Building, the lake through the trees, valley beyond. I rose muttering I wasn't a fuckin' pioneer.

We got one pole up. There was nothing fragile about that lone pole; it was a severe single object. Began work on the next one.

"Hold it, I'll go up," Dan said.

I held it in place, hammer in hand, while Dan walked up a ways in the Pasture. I was afraid.

"To your left — more. Okay — no, back to your left."

I hit the nail — tentative. Nothing happened. I hit it again and felt it had gone some.

"The other one," Dan called. "Try and have them go in together."

I hit the other, and then again: returned to the first one, hit it and it bent. Dan called for me to wait, and walked down. I was furious, frustrated, grim with anger.

"It's all in the eye," he said. "Focus on the head of the nail. Don't think about anything. You have a good eye: fix it on the head of the nail, and swing."

He put his hand on my shoulder, and chuckled. "I don't know if I told you, but it has to be ready when the crop comes in."

I gripped the hammer and nodded. He showed me how to straighten the nail, saying this probably won't work with oak, but anyway...

The nail bends into an upside down L shape, and using a little leverage, with the claw of the hammer, it can be straightened, but the kink it will leave marks the point at which it will bend again, and if the nail is over an inch in oak it can't be removed except by the kind of forced hard work that defeats itself, so the workman, in a rage, flattens the nail to one side, down against the surface, which is impossible with oak because the spring of the nail, opposed by the power in oak, prevents the nail from being flattened down, it bounces back, stays just off the surface: the nail is the loser for the nail is resilient, not the wood.

I worried the nail out, it had hardly gone in, started a new one and did manage, as Dan guided me from the distance, to keep the pole straight. He walked down and we began on number three, as I said, my face covered with sweat.

"Those rat bastards cut this with machine saws: *they* didn't have to work with it."

He said, "They dragged it down by tractor and cut it up. But I wonder...what a knot in oak will do to the teeth of a mechanical saw."

"Oh I sympathize with them."

He smiled, "Technology creeps on."

We were a little tense.

We got the third pole up, the fourth and the day was done. We put the tools in the keg, and walked down. Beat.

Passed Doyle's house: he was puttering around the side yard. It was impossible not to say a civil hello. We stopped, and Doyle smiled hello, looked Dan straight in the eyes.

"How's that Tobacco Barn coming?"

"Slow."

"If you need more nails, let me know."

We nodded. I said, "We probably will."

Doyle made a sudden loud laugh. "You're damned RIGHT you will," and slapped me on the back, and shouted, "Oh boy! That's OAK!"

We three laughed. I sheepish: he laughed again,

"Hey Fee, how do you like that GODDAMNED OAK!"

Southerners repeated themselves, and he, still laughing, said,

"That oak is gonna *teach* you."

Dan moved away. It was over: we said so long, and crossed the potato field to the bridge. Doyle's eyes had flashed with the word teach, and Dan was frowning.

"He sure has it bad," he said.

I nodded. Sorry. "We worked so well together."

Dan didn't say anything — if he would have it would have been, "It's too late for that, Fee." The political infighting had overcome the memories of the many months before: the fifteen hour days Doyle and I had worked, side by side, to part in darkness after all the silage was in, slap each other on the shoulder affectionately, murmur goodnight and head for home. Claire, his wife, would call, asking me in for coffee, or cold homebrew: some evenings I went, but most not, because of concerts, I had to go down the mountain and shower and shave, and change…all that was no more: even with me Doyle's hostility couldn't be suppressed: he was so antagonistic to Olson. I was suspect.

And too bad. Farm work is the hardest, cleanest, most rewarding work there is. My memories of Doyle with his wife and their son are vivid, and sad, for yet another aspect of the school, long forgotten or ignored. She made the sweetest butter I ever tasted.

We passed the house that later burned, remembering how I had gazed at Motherwell's bright mural night after night coming back from farm work, July, two and a half years before. I used to gaze and gaze at the bright colors, standing in the darkness outside. Once I saw him, studying it and puffing on a cigarette.

We passed the house where Charley taught his Shakespeare class, and where Dan would have his studio when I was in the Army: told me later he had been painting hard and long, one night, and it got late, suddenly feeling he was being watched, he turned, and in the extended shaft of light, a fox crouched in the doorway, looking at him.

We crossed the bridge where Charley had turned his back on me when I said Lear too was nature — as well as Antony & Cleopatra. We passed the Studies Building, and walked down the road to the Dininghall for supper.

A few days later all the poles were up, and we began on the one by five planks across the top.

The first horizontal was put up by lifting it and laying it on the flat tops of the poles, in such a way as to leave margin there for the following plank. The first couple were the most difficult — they *all* were. I can't remember if we put middle horizontal beams in. I don't remember.* Getting the poles up was task enough, we lay the board across the top and climbed up an angled temporary plank, hoisted ourselves up and straddled the loose top plank. Hair raising work since both ends of the plank were resting on a couple of inches halving the circle of the top of the pole, so when we got up there, a chore in itself for me, we had to sit still, and if a need to adjust position, it had to be done carefully else the plank would slip and we would fall, and certainly hurt ourselves, one of us sliding down astride the rough plank, the other falling freely, depending which end slipped first. We straddled the beam back to back, facing away from each other. We couldn't think about it. If we did think we couldn't hit the nails straight, the nerve-wracking thing was if the plank slipped, it would be a very sudden — complete surprise.

We were proud of what we had already done. We had used the

---

*We did, before we put the top pieces on. The structure was a series of H shapes. The middle beams were a nightmare to put in: we hammered sideways. Afterwards, though, it was easier to climb up on top.

No. After we had the uprights fixed, we nailed bottom boards or planks between the uprights, all along the foundation. Thus they were toed in. We next put the top beams on because the poles were so wobbly. Then we put in the middle. While doing the rewrite of this I phoned Dan, and asked him. (11/5/89) level to check out the vertical poles. Every pole was straight. In that wonderful glassed in concavity, that little bubble in the green fluid rested between the black hairlines exactly: on the last pole Dan and I looked at each other.

We had built the initial part of the superstructure by eye, and it was perfect.

We sat up there in the sky, astride the wobbly plank, myself to one end, Dan to the other, hammering away.

My right hand had flattened, and holding it against my left I saw my fingers were wider, had spread from repeated concussion: the soft parts of my fingers, on the inner side between the joints were flat, hard, and glossy: all blisters had gone, I felt a power in my grip, in my wrist, arm, shoulder and back that I hadn't felt since baseball days in high school when I pitched. But still — the beginning with every nail, it was such a long way from the nailhead to the plank — five inches, five feet — forget about that sweet sensation of nailing into pine, approaching the end as the nail zips down into the wood you open up, and when the nail is in you give that final shot, or, like Franz used to, four or five final shots whap whapwhap WHAM done. But with oak, if a quarter inch of a nail was sticking up, and the hammer blow was off, the nail would bend, and exactly at the surface, the nail, so imbedded, so gripped by the oak, rather slipped to one side, and stayed, tilt. It was all incredible. The shocker — the dangerous and most surprising shock was, upon setting the nail, to begin it, on the first hard downward smack, hit just off target in a special way, often, the sound was a sharp zing, but brittle, a squeak, a scream from the nail, and it flashed out, flew up near our faces, to sail away, sound ringing in our ears.

We seldom spoke except for outcries of rage, and on my part a sudden furious smashing down on a bent nail. The intensity of the labor, the act: two of us apart, yet together in the effort — my left hand gripping the edge of the plank, my eye crystallizing the nailhead, not tempted by the two or three bent nails surrounding it, and the rising up of my arm, tilt of my head, the arching of my back and the swift downward swing of hammer and the neat full smack in the true strike, and then again, watching the nailhead, knowing the nail was, blow by blow, sinking into that oak, and in finishing up one end of one board, to anchor one end of another, we changed positions, so that we faced each other: a few inches away from my nail, Dan was working on his nail — two figures, facing each other, swinging hammers up there, on top on the mountainside.*

He handed up the next plank, and on tip toe swung it into place on the next pole top, while I slid it in place at my fingertips, and went to work, holding the nail with my left hand while the hammer drove the nail into starting place. With the glitter of the nailhead in my eye, I removed my left hand, and gripped the edge of the plank. My mind charted my arm and the full down swing, the hit, and I lifted my arm. I worked and sweated, swung, hit, swung, hit.

I peered down at the nail. What had happened? It — it was a strange color of lead and violet. I yelled,

"The Goddamned thing's changed color!"

I looked across at Dan — it was dark! I heard his hammer hit.

"Hey!" I shouted. "Let's quit! For Christ's sake — it's NIGHT!"

I saw his dim figure look up. "Well by God, so it is."

"Beautiful."

"It is," he agreed.

---

*Once, however, the exasperation and frustration came to a head. Dan and I arrived on the site, and for some reason I thought the saw was in the corner, at the base of the foundation: it wasn't there. I asked him where it was, we weren't using it then, but I thought it was there, no, he said, it was over there: he pointed. But yesterday it was here, I said. No, it wasn't, he said. It was, I insisted, we left it here yesterday. Dan became angry, and said we had not. I stammered, shaken and defensive, that we *had* left the saw there. Yesterday, in fact I had seen it. His face reddened. He pivoted, and ran, hopping over debris, until he came to a spot where he bent, picked up the saw, held it aloft, and cried,

"Here — HERE is your saw!"

It stood in the Pasture against the line of distant trees, against the late afternoon sky.

We were standing about a hundred and fifty feet down from it. Our part of it was finished. Its structure was simple. It was strong, and firm in its place. As we walked away I turned for one more look.

The upright oak poles were straight, and the middle beams, and flat oak planks across the top gave it classic form. The sense of my having put half the nails in it, made it mine, and that I knew every nail, made me proud. I caught up with Dan, and heard him mutter bitterly,

"Now those fatheads can come up and ruin it."

Which they did. They put cross beams and cross braces, a couple hundred more nails and a roof like an upside down Viking ship on, with more braces and beams and nails. It couldn't hold, they said. It had too many open places.

That was my last fall season at Black Mountain.

Yet it, and the last complete year was the dream. From the fall of 1952, to the summer of '53, especially the very early and late spring.

I met my most beautiful girl in January. Her soft tapping on my door betokened her desire for me, almost broke my heart: her coming into my arms, and on to my filthy sheets on my little mattress for our nights of sex and sleep, made me almost dizzy with pride and guilt and affection and fear and elation.

During the spring of '53, Charley Egan's gallery had a four man exhibition at the Woman's College, in Greensboro: Franz, Philip, Jack Tworkov, George NcNeil, and Charley Egan went down for a couple of days, and then drove across state to visit Black Mountain. Those few days were paradise to me. I had seen a Container Corporation ad in Time Magazine, a water color Philip had done in Italy — I had loved it, and of course told him. He and Jack and Franz were enthusiastic about my new drawing of the girls, and of course we talked and talked and drank and drank and played some softball.

J.P. Grady generally umpired these games: but he played right field, and Charley Egan umpired. Olson played first base, Joel pitched, Franz played second, did I play shortstop, or left field? Dan played third base, he threw to first like striking a match on the sidewalk, and the ball soared over Charley's hands into the rhododendron by the lake.

"Damn!" Dan yelled, throwing his glove on the ground.

I wondered why he didn't throw sidearm.

Jorge was in centerfield. The other team, it's hard to return to so many — Harvey, Jonathan, Joe Fiore, Jack Rice, the girls, Elaine Chamberlain later, Betty Motherwell, the girl who ran away to South America, Joan Heller — were good, plus Jack Boyd, Jay Watt, Bill what'shisname who really pasted my slow pitch...but I struck out Jonathan, at will, telling him I was going to strike him out when he came to bat.

"Pitch the ball, citizen," he laughed. "Don't lecture me."

We ran around the bases, threw the ball everywhere but where it was supposed to go...the memory of Franz missing a throw — he dove up, hands outstretched, yet together like a diver, as the ball zipped into right field he came down frowning that he had missed it, while Egan laughed.

In this spirit, a story must be told, again, the great story which has never been told right, except by Franz, that in East Hampton, the day after the party when Elaine deKooning dipped hundreds of pennies into gold paint, let them dry and sprinkled them across the lawn, and Nancy and Joan tied was it balloons to the trees, and later Elaine, for the game the next day — if this isn't right, it is anyway — she painted two — two — grapefruits white, painted the stitches around, and the Spaulding mark on each, and the next day in the game, with Vincente pitching, Franz catching, and Philip Pavia at bat, Franz, in the pretense of going out to the mound for a little conference slipped one of the white grapefruits to Vincente, and returned behind the plate.

Everybody, Franz told me, knew but Pavia. The players on both teams, the kids, the wives, the girl friends — deKooning doubled up in laughter in centerfield, Vincente threw, Pavia swung, and hit —

"All right," he said, after the mess was cleaned up and everybody calmed down, "let's play."

"Just a second," Franz said, "I want to talk to Vincente."

During a game in Provincetown, years later, the bases were loaded and I was at bat. Franz was pitching. I told the left fielder and the center fielder to move back: they didn't so I hit the ball over the left fielder's head, and because the field was so big, I was around third base by the time he picked up the ball. In the same inning I came to bat and yelled for the left fielder and center fielder to move back, which they did.

"Aw hit the fuckin' ball," Franz griped.

I waved my bat over the plate. "You put it where I want it and I'll hit it."

He threw a couple of low ones. I held out my hand at chest height, over the center of the plate.

He put it right there and I hit it over the center fielder's head, and crossed the plate as he picked up the ball. I was looking at Franz. He didn't like it at all, affected an expression that he was sick of me.

When their visit was over, that spring, there was a triumph in me. Black Mountain had become two schools, one of New York and the men above: the other — Charley's Black Mountain.

They got in McNeil's station wagon. Franz and Charley lowered the tailgate and they got on, and sat legs dangling. I faced them. The car was parked in front of the Dininghall under the

tree, by the millstone. I took Franz's hand and our eyes met. I said so long: he said,
"Write me."
"I will."
I shook hands with Charley Egan: in his ball cap, the prototype of the umpire, smiling,
"Good meeting you, Fee."
In the cries of farewell from the crowd gathering around, the car began to move forward. I walked with it a little, and as it went slowly because of the gutted dirt road, I was able to go a little distance with it. I began to walk faster, and then run. Franz moved to his left, Egan moved to his right, and they patted the space between and laughed,
"C'mon Fee, get on. Come with us — "
I — I ran — but...
The car gathered speed, passed the ballfield and tennis court, and as it passed the little bungalow by the white fence, and turned out onto the asphalt road, Franz and Egan waved.
I waved back.

I wrote Franz that spring vacation was coming up, and could I visit him in New York. Did he have a cot, or something, could I stay in the back of his loft...he wrote back sure, come ahead, and I wrote my mother the news.

I went, but had to return sooner than I wanted. I had an interview with a judge in Asheville: late April. My protest had been rejected, I was classified 1A, and would go in the Army. In late July the Korean Truce was signed. *Whew!*

I was glad, but still frightened and anxious, yet — I had moments of power, my anxiety of departing from the places I had loved was a true heightened sense of loss. The places, the bright circles.

On a warm, late spring afternoon the sky was cloudy, a dark dirty gray, very low on the mountain: gathering since lunchtime, and towards supper a strange wet breeze appeared, and as I stood on the Dininghall porch by the lake, watching students and faculty walk down the road from the Studies Building, I heard a light, and then heavier, pattering on the roof. The figures began to run. Small hailstones quickly began to cover the ground, but in the sky they were getting larger: small hailstones were consolidating, and from the size of the chickpeas, they became clusters of golfball size, and then the size of baseballs, and finally, the lake looking like it was being shelled, great geyser spouts leaped up, and the noise was deafening on the Dininghall roof — Bert dashed out and got one, and holding it in my hand on the porch, I saw its structure. It was the size of a grapefruit, composed of dozens of little hailstones, a dense and opaque milk/crystal color, slightly like hominy. The distant sound of them crashing through trees, the repeating dull thumps as they hit the muddy edges of the lake, and the racket on the roof was like being under bombardment. One of the faculty rushed in saying they had come through the roof of his convertible. Bert and I put one in the freezer to keep.

A summer evening rain gathering behind the mountain, and I can see the man yet, a faculty member, coming out of the Office, walking towards the Dininghall. I was on the small front porch by the tree and the millstone, and I cried out for him to hurry. He looked over his shoulder and began to run. A gray and silver wall of rain came down the mountain full force, the ground darkened behind him, I held the door open, he flashed by with a laugh of alarm, the rain hit the building like a hard slap, and swept across the lake, and the valley, leaving rivers, creeks and pools in its wake.

THE LOST YOUNG MAN

Walking in thought around the lake by the Dininghall I saw a young man, bare headed, in slacks, dusty shoes, white shirt, and a sports jacket on his arm walk up the road empty-handed, looking around. I crossed the grass to him.

Introduced myself, he murmured his name and we shook hands and sat on the cool grass by the lake. He was moved by the beauty. Across the lake the long white ship of the Studies Building gleamed against the trees and tall grass by the water, low against the mountain. I asked,

"Where are you from?"

He looked at me. "I've been traveling around," he murmured...sad.

"What's around — like where?"

"Oh," he paused. "You know. Here and there..."

I rose and said let's go get a peanut butter sandwich and some milk. He brightened, and we went into the kitchen. I introduced him to Malrey and Corny — the cooks, and made sandwiches, poured cold blue milk, fresh that morning, and he and I went out and sat at a table on the porch and faced the lake. One of Stefan's students was rehearsing piano in the Round House, just off the Dininghall. The young man gazed out over the lake for a moment, and turned to me.

"It's breathtaking."

His face shone. He chewed his sandwich slowly, he had been hungry all right, and he talked, a little, while he chewed. He said he had hitchhiked all over the country, aimlessly, he admitted, because he didn't know what to do, or where to go, had seen the small wooden sign on a pole by the highway, had heard of the school before, so he turned off to come to see it. I nodded, rolled two cigarettes, which amused him, as did my tanned near naked body. I lit the cigarettes and we sat back puffing and loving the splendor before us. In silence, to the distant piano music.

After a while I asked him if he'd like to take a ride on the raft, and he thought that was funny, but we did. Sitting out in the middle of the lake, I could see the effect working, and he began to talk.

"I had a bad experience," he began. "The War, my—boat, the torpedo boat I was on got lost — I don't remember much of it, except the wandering, we drifted around the Pacific, just floated around, the days were — long, and the weeks, we floated on and on..."

I poled the raft over to the dam, and we sat on a corner in the shade: he said, with a smile,

"I wish I knew what to do."

He stayed for supper, and that night I got a pillow case, a couple of sheets and a light blanket, showed him where he'd sleep, and pointed out the bathroom and showers, said breakfast was from eight until ten, I think. Maybe it was seven to nine.

The next morning we had breakfast together — I had introduced him around the day before, so when the table filled with students, he wasn't too alarmed. M.C. sat with us, and we drank coffee as she—gentle—explained the school was broke, and though he could stay a few days, it was really impossible for him to stay any longer. He nodded, and said of course.

The next couple of days while I was in classes he saw the farm, climbed the mountain, came to one of Charley's classes, and watched Katy's dance class from a far corner, unnoticed, in the Dininghall. He was impressed by our seriousness, and as he lay in the grass near the Office, which was across the road from the Dininghall, reading, barefoot, no shirt on, a point of light had appeared in his eyes, and we talked about things. He had been born and brought up in Illinois, finished high school, joined the Navy to beat the Army draft: after the war was in a hospital a while, and after being released, began wandering around.

He liked the farm, and the mountain.

The afternoon of the fourth day, he left: we chipped in and gave him a couple of dollars, a sack of Durham, and a few flowers. One of the girls and I made up a couple of sandwiches, a tomato and some radishes and wrapped them in wax paper and put it all in a bag...I walked down the rocky road with him, we talked a little, and on the asphalt road by the entrance, we shook hands. I wished him good luck, and he thanked me and asked that I thank everyone. I said I would. After he had gone a way, he turned. We waved goodbye, and seeing him standing in the middle of that country road, I remembered a book I had read when I was a boy, I remembered the man in the picture at the end, one hand on his heart and the other raised in a gesture of farewell, as he left the land where the bees live.

(Spring 1941 Tuesday   Dear Fee —

It is always good to hear from you and your last letter was a dandy.

I think it is mighty good of Jean to let you ride her horse and I'm glad you are learning to ride. Maybe when you grow up you will be a Pony Express rider.

Are you playing lots of baseball? I'm glad you like your glove and I'll get you a finger mitt next time if that is what you want. I listen to the ball game almost every afternoon over the radio.

Did you know they played baseball in the Bible? I used to know a song about it — like this —

> Eve stole first
> And Adam stole second
> And Satan umpired the game.
> Rebecca went to the wall with the pitcher
> Out on the field of fame
> Goliath was struck out by David
> And a base hit was made by Cain
> The Prodigal Son made one home run
> Brother Noah gave out checks for rain.

I'm glad you are doing well in school and I guess you will be pretty glad when vacation comes
With lots of love
>Signing off
>[Take it away McCloskey]
>Dad)

February, 1942

We had watery hash and rice for lunch, and when I met mother after school I felt funny. On the drive out to the Veteran's Hospital she let me have a smoke, but I didn't feel right.

We went down the corridor and up the elevator, down another corridor in that acrid hospital smell: we entered the room. He was in the first bed to the left.

I shook hands with him, but he gestured, with a wink, to wait, he was listening to the ballgame on an earset, telling me the play as it was happening: Creepy Crespi, the Cardinal shortstop, went behind second towards right field, got the hard grounder, somersaulted, and with his feet in the air, threw to first for the out, the Cards were out of the inning.

My father's right side was paralyzed from head to foot: his right temple was swollen with tumor. Ugly. The doctors kept cutting the growth off. The red scars were hideous. His face was crooked. He held my hand with his left hand, and we talked. I told him about school, and baseball. But he tired. Mother talked with him in a tender superficial way, with an inner tone I didn't understand that made me angry, and anxious.

My eyes began to tear, my hands trembled at my side and my father's eye showed alarm, as mother came around the bed. I was salivating, and as she made the turn, my eyes blurred, my stomach heaved — I buckled forward at the waist as my hands rose to my mouth. My father struggled helplessly to come to me, the vomit charged up my throat, I couldn't breathe. It gushed out of my nose and mouth, poured out, coughing and choking and weeping, with it down my shirt, in my hands, on my short pants and shoes, and on the floor as my mother held me I gagged on bits of food. An attendant half picked me up, and helped me to a cot in the next room: mother washed my face and hands and legs. I rested a while.

I asked for a glass of water, my throat on fire, and the water, cooling me, was good at first, and cleared my head, and I felt I could return to his bedside, yet no sooner than I began towards him, the convulsions returned anew, the water turned to acid, and rose mixed with the residue of food, it streamed from my mouth and nose, I gagged and coughed and dribbled, as mother, very worried again held me, while I wept.

April 4th, 1942
CLARENCE DAWSON BURIED HERE MON.
Husband of Cara Byars Dawson
Succumbs After Long Illness

I stood beside mother and gazed, dry-eyed, at my father's face in the casket. His skull was waxen, scarred, and ugly. I turned away.

"That's not my father."

It was a cool rainy day, and as the funeral cortege drove across town to the cemetery, I looked out the window at April trees, and lawns and houses and passing cars. The air was fresh and damp, as was the earth where he went.

At home, afterwards, in the drape-drawn Victorian living room my mother sat in an upholstered chair and drank a glass of sherry. I sat across the room from her, watching my aunts stare at the floor. One of my aunts told me, and she was the *first:* that I would have to be a good boy.

I hit the ball with a fine swing. It took off high right away, and before reaching zenith cleared the top of the tree by inches, and kept on going. As the outfielders got it I crossed home plate, looking at Hitler who was clapping his hands. I sat beside him. It was the longest ball ever hit at Black Mountain.

March–September 1967
New York

Photo: Mimi Fronczak

FIELDING DAWSON was born in New York in 1930. Grew up in the Midwest, went to Black Mountain College from 1949 until 1953 when he was drafted. After serving in the Army he settled in New York, where he still lives. Is the author of 19 published books, a member of P.E.N. and Chairman of the P.E.N. Prison Writing Committee. He is an exhibiting artist, a Pantheon author, and belongs to the Democratic Socialists of America.

Typeset by The Typewright (Lexington, Kentucky) in Adobe Garamond. Printed by Thomson-Shore, Inc. Design by Jonathan Greene.